THIS DIARY BELONGS TO

....

2022
Astrology
Diary

patsy Bennett

A Rockpool book
PO Box 252
Summer Hill
NSW 2130
Australia

rockpoolpublishing.co
Follow us! **f** ⓞ rockpoolpublishing
Tag your images with #rockpoolpublishing

ISBN: 9781925946321
Northern hemisphere edition

Published in 2021, by Rockpool Publishing
Copyright text © Patsy Bennett, 2021
Copyright design © Rockpool Publishing 2021

Internal design by Jessica Le, Rockpool Publishing
Cover design by Sara Lindberg, Rockpool Publishing
Typesetting by Adala Group
Edited by Lisa Macken
Frontispiece by W.G. Evans, 1856, Map of the Constellations in July, August, September.
Other map illustrations by Alexander Jamieson, 1822, Celestial Atlas.
Glyph illustrations by http://All-Silhouettes.com
Zodiac illustrations by http://vectorian.net
Compass illustration by Jessica Le, Rockpool Publishing

Printed and bound in China
10 9 8 7 6 5 4 3 2 1

NB: the planetary phenomena and aspects listed on each day are set to
Greenwich Meantime (GMT) apart from the summer time (27 March
to 30 October), where they are set to British Summer Time. To convert
times to your locations please see www.timeanddate.com. Astrological
interpretations take into account all aspects and the sign the sun and
planets are in on each day and are not taken out of context.

introduction

Make 2022 your best year yet! This is a year of great transformation, one where being adaptable rather than inflexible will help you move ahead. It will be an important year in your journey, a year in which you'll feel encouraged to reach out and explore new and exciting options.

This diary/planner is designed to help you to make the most of your year. If you live your life by the sun, moon and stars you'll love the *2022 Astrology Diary*: you'll have expert astrological advice right at your fingertips! I have interpreted major daily astrological data for you to help you to plan ahead, so that 2022 will be all you wish it to be and you can enjoy the days. Refer to 'How to use this diary' for more details about the terminology used in the diary pages.

The major strategies for personal growth and success this year are:

- Be practical and realistic.
- Be adaptable rather than obstinate.
- Manage strong emotions.
- Be the calm in the storm.
- Focus on nurturance, both of yourself and others.

There is an exciting feeling to this year, as you will discover new gifts and talents and find ways to surge ahead with skill sets you already have and to learn more.

April, May, October and November will signal true turning points and may be super intense, so ensure you follow a steady and stable path this year so you can navigate potentially far-reaching changes.

Mid-year there will be a chance to review and recap the actions you took earlier in the year, so don't be afraid to instigate new plans, work projects and personal initiatives as you can rearrange and review them from mid-year onwards.

Jupiter, the planet that brings abundance and opportunities, will be travelling through Pisces and Aries all year. This transit will help you to expand your repertoire and your influence on and impact in life. The process will initially offer you the chance in the first quarter of the year to dig deep into the recesses of your soul and to retrieve information and wisdom that you need to surge ahead to create a more abundant life. Then, from May to July when Jupiter is in Aries, it will be a particularly favourable time to put adventurous plans into action.

A reflective mood from August to the end of the year, when Jupiter will be largely retrograde, will enable you to tie up loose threads and/or reorientate your plans and thoughts so they better mesh with prevailing trends and cultural and social circumstances.

As the moon's north node steps into grounded and practical Taurus in January there will be less chop and change and the chance to build solid structures in your life. A priority will be to find security, stability and nurturance; however, as the moon's nodes square Saturn in early April and approach unpredictable Uranus mid-year, expect a change of focus and the need to rethink some of your practices such as work and long-term goals.

A major conjunction this year will be that of Jupiter and Neptune in mid-April. This could bring your greatest hopes and projects to fruition, but if you tend to overestimate your abilities and skill sets this conjunction could put focus on areas of your life in which you have lacked diligence with your preparation and research. Jupiter conjunct Neptune can bring your greatest hopes into being, but it can also spotlight the areas of your life you have misjudged and bring a sense of deep disillusionment. So if you prepare your aims and goals early on in 2022 you could truly make wonderful progress.

The eclipses in 2022 will be across the Taurus/Scorpio axis, bringing most change this year to these two signs and to those with a significant Taurus or Scorpio signature in your chart, such as a rising sign, moon's node, mid-heaven, moon sign or planetary placement. As well, fellow fixed signs Leo and Aquarius will experience the most changes in 2022.

The eclipse seasons will be in April-May and October-November, and you'll experience an opportunity for great personal growth and to make long-overdue changes in your life at these times. These phases may be particularly intense, so ensure you build strong character and resilience that enables you to move forward both with a stable outlook and in practical terms. Aim to build a sense of personal strength early in the year so you are able and ready to tackle change as it arises.

To feel you are moving in the right direction it's important to feel fulfilled by what you do in your everyday life. This year's conjunction of the moon's north node and Uranus on 31 July will potentially alter what – and who – makes you happy, so be prepared to look outside the box at what will make you happy while being safe in the knowledge that you are a developing person and the path you tread has many twists and turns.

Developments at the end of July/early August will bring into sharp focus the fact that what makes you happy will also change over time. Be prepared, however, to maintain the highest principles and values, or this year you risk being blown off course and may even succumb to behaviour you would not usually endorse in anyone else, let alone in yourself.

Another prevailing aspect in 2022 will be the Saturn/Uranus 'square' aspect (90 degrees), further adding tension to developments in the bigger picture, both socially and economically in the world. You may find you experience tension in your own life from the point of view that new ideas and projects seem hard to put in place, especially at the new year and then once more in October and November.

The key to making the most of this tough aspect between Saturn and Uranus is to find ways to build a strong framework for your endeavours while being open to new skill sets and ideas you can learn, so that effectively you can build fresh, strong foundations on top of an already existing solid framework for your endeavours moving forward.

You must be adaptable in this regard and avoid hanging on to the past for little or no reason such as sentimentality or habit. This process may be challenging, but you will find that if you do not work with change then change tends to seemingly work against your best interests. So be proactive in 2022; do not leave everything to fate. And remember: you make your own luck.

The motto for 2022? *Be proactive and embrace change.*

how to use this diary

Solar, lunar and planetary movements

This diary lists the major solar, planetary and lunar movements day by day, and I have interpreted these so you can plan your days, weeks and months according to prevailing astrological trends. You'll gain insight into which days will be favourable for your planned events – from important meetings, get-togethers and celebrations to trips and life decisions – and which days will be variable may even be frustrating. You'll see, when you plan your life by the stars, that sometimes taking ill-timed action can lead to disappointment and that taking well-timed action will lead to success.

The sun in the zodiac signs

Astrology is the study of the movement of celestial objects from our point of view here on earth. We are most familiar with the study of our sun signs, which depicts the movement and placement of the sun in the zodiac signs Aries through to Pisces. In the same way the sun moves through the zodiac signs Aries to Pisces through the calendar year, so do the planets and other celestial objects such as asteroid planet Chiron.

This diary features monthly forecasts when the sun is in each sign, beginning with the sun in Capricorn (December 2021 to January 2022) and proceeding through the signs and finishing once again with the sun in Capricorn in December 2022.

Each monthly forecast applies to everyone, as it is a general forecast for all sun signs. There is also a forecast uniquely for your own particular sun sign, thus you'll find the 'For Capricorn' section is uniquely for Capricorns and so on. When the sun is in your own sign it can prove particularly motivational and is a great time to get ahead with projects that resonate with your self-esteem, gut instincts and bigger-picture motivation.

The moon in the zodiac signs

Just as the sun moves through the zodiac signs, so does the moon. This diary lists these movements, as they can have a perceived influence over the mood and tone of the day, just as the sun in different signs is known to characterise different traits. Where a diary entry states 'The moon enters Taurus', this indicates that the moon has left the zodiac sign Aries and has entered the sign of Taurus and will now reside in Taurus until it moves on to Gemini in a couple of days' time.

New moons and full moons are also listed in this diary, as these can mark turning points within your journey through the year. New moons are generally a great time to begin a new project. Full moons can signify a culmination or a peak in a project or event, so if you're planning to launch a business or your children wish to begin a new course or activity you can check in this diary if the day you're planning your event will be favourable for beginning a fresh venture. Simply check to see if your new venture falls on or near a new moon, and also take a look at the diary entries either side of your proposed events to ensure celestial influences will be working in your favour.

Eclipses can indicate particularly powerful turning points, and it is for this reason eclipses are also listed in the diary dates. If a lunar or solar eclipse is in the same sign as your own particular sun sign it may be particularly potent.

The phases of the moon can truly influence the tone of your day, so this diary features every moon sign, daily. The moon remains in each sign for approximately two days. Below is listed the mood depending on which sign the moon is in on a daily basis.

MOON IN ARIES: can bring an upbeat approach to life, but restlessness or fiery outbursts can result if you or those around you feel they are under pressure.

MOON IN TAURUS: can bring stability to feelings and routine, a sensual time and predilection for all things artistic and musical, but over-indulgence and stubbornness can result if you are under pressure.

MOON IN GEMINI: can bring a chatty, talkative approach to life, but flippancy, indecision and uncertainty can result if you or those around you feel under pressure.

MOON IN CANCER: a sense of security, nesting, cocooning and nurturance will be sought for family time and those you love, but in securities or a lack of adaptability can result if you feel you are under pressure.

MOON IN LEO: an upbeat approach to life and more dynamic attitude to others and yourself will arise, but a Leo moon can bring arrogance, pride and vanity to the surface if you are under pressure.

MOON IN VIRGO: a great time to focus on health, routine, decluttering, work and being helpful, but over-analysis, obsessive attention to detail and ambivalence can also arise if you are under pressure.

MOON IN LIBRA: a lovely time to focus on art, music, love, creating harmony and peace, but a sense of disharmony, indecision and dissatisfaction can arise if you're under pressure.

MOON IN SCORPIO: a time for focusing on personal needs, sensuality, enjoyment of life and indulgence in all things wonderful, but if you are under pressure deep feelings can emerge that are intense or potentially destructive.

MOON IN SAGITTARIUS: an outgoing, upbeat phase when an adventurous attitude will bring out your joviality and lust for learning and life. When you are under pressure, you and others may appear blunt or disregard the feelings of other people.

MOON IN CAPRICORN: can stimulate a practical and focused approach to work and to your goals and plans. But when you are under pressure a sense of limitations, restrictions and authoritarian strictures can arise.

MOON IN AQUARIUS: a quirky, outgoing phase during which trying new activities and new approaches to life will appeal. When you're under pressure the moon in Aquarius may stimulate unreliability, unconventionality or changeability.

MOON IN PISCES: a dreamy, introverted or artistic time in which music, the arts and romance will thrive. A good time for meditation. When you're under pressure a Pisces moon can bring excessive daydreaming, forgetfulness or vagueness.

NB: if you know your moon sign you may find that when the moon is in your sign, as listed in this diary, life is either easier or more challenging depending on the planetary aspects to your moon at the time of your birth. Keep a note of the general mood or occurrences when the moon is in your sign and you may find that a pattern emerges.

Interplanetary aspects

Astrologers study the movements of planets in relation to each other. The measurements, which are in degrees, minutes and seconds, focus on patterns and particular aspects, which are the angles between the planets, the sun and other celestial objects. This diary includes mention of these aspects between the sun and the planets, and the terminology used is explained below – from 'opposition' (when a planet is opposite another) to 'quincunx' (when a planet is at a 150-degree angle to another).

The angles the planets and the sun make to one another have meanings in astrology. For example, a 'trine' aspect (120-degree angle) can be considered beneficial for the progress of your plans, while a 'square' aspect (90-degree angle) can present as a challenge (depending on your own attitude to challenges and obstacles).

By choosing dates carefully for the fruition of your plans you will be moving forward with the benefit of the knowledge of the cosmic influences that can help your progress.

NB: when you read the planetary aspects in this diary such as 'Sun square Uranus' be aware that the aspect's influence may span to a day before and a day after the actual date it is entered in this diary, especially regarding outer planets (Neptune, Uranus and Pluto). However, the moon phases are relevant for each day.

Planetary aspects

CONJUNCTION: when a celestial object is at the same degree and generally in the same sign of the zodiac as another celestial object and therefore is aligned from our point of view here on earth. This can intensify the dynamics between the celestial objects and earth.

OPPOSITION: when a planet is opposite another, at a 180-degree angle. This can intensify the interplanetary dynamics.

SEXTILE: a 60-degree angle. This can be a peaceful, harmonious influence or facilitate the flow of energy between planetary influences.

SEMI-SEXTILE: a 30-degree angle. This is a harmonious aspect or facilitates the flow of energy between planetary influences.

SQUARE: a 90-degree angle. This can be a challenging aspect, but as some people get going when the going gets tough it can lead to a breakthrough.

TRINE: a 120-degree angle. This can be a peaceful, harmonious influence or facilitate the flow of energy between planetary influences.

QUINCUNX: a 150-degree angle. This can present a hurdle to be overcome.

Retrogrades

Planets can appear to go backwards from our point of view here on earth. The best-known retrograde phases are those of Mercury and Venus, although all other planets also turn retrograde and these retrograde phases are mentioned in this diary.

Retrograde phases can be a good time to assimilate, consolidate and integrate recent developments, although traditionally retrograde phases are associated with delays, a slow down or difficult process. For example, a Mercury retrograde phase is often associated with difficult communications or traffic snarls, yet it can be an excellent time to integrate events and consolidate, review and reorder your ideas. This diary lists the start and finish dates of Mercury retrograde phases, as well as the kinds of activities that may be influenced by this phenomenon.

A 'station' is when planets turn from one direction to the other from our point of view here on earth.

JANUARY

S	M	T	W	T	F	S
30	31					1
2	3	4	5	6	7	8
9	10	11	12	13	14	15
16	17	18	19	20	21	22
23	24	25	26	27	28	29

FEBRUARY

S	M	T	W	T	F	S
		1	2	3	4	5
6	7	8	9	10	11	12
13	14	15	16	17	18	19
20	21	22	23	24	25	26
27	28					

MARCH

S	M	T	W	T	F	S
		1	2	3	4	5
6	7	8	9	10	11	12
13	14	15	16	17	18	19
20	21	22	23	24	25	26
27	28	29	30	31		

APRIL

S	M	T	W	T	F	S
					1	2
3	4	5	6	7	8	9
10	11	12	13	14	15	16
17	18	19	20	21	22	23
24	25	26	27	28	29	30

MAY

S	M	T	W	T	F	S
1	2	3	4	5	6	7
8	9	10	11	12	13	14
15	16	17	18	19	20	21
22	23	24	25	26	27	28
29	30	31				

JUNE

S	M	T	W	T	F	S
			1	2	3	4
5	6	7	8	9	10	11
12	13	14	15	16	17	18
19	20	21	22	23	24	25
26	27	28	29	30		

2022 NORTHERN HEMISPHERE MOON PHASES

JULY

S	M	T	W	T	F	S
31					1	2
☽					☽	☽
3	4	5	6	7	8	9
☽	☽	☽	●	●	●	●
10	11	12	13	14	15	16
●	●	●	●	●	●	●
17	18	19	20	21	22	23
●	●	●	●	◖	◖	◖
24	25	26	27	28	29	30
◖	◖	◖	◖	○	☽	☽

AUGUST

S	M	T	W	T	F	S
	1	2	3	4	5	6
	☽	☽	☽	◗	◑	●
7	8	9	10	11	12	13
●	●	●	●	●	●	●
14	15	16	17	18	19	20
●	●	●	●	●	◖	◖
21	22	23	24	25	26	27
◖	◖	◖	◖	◖	◖	○
28	29	30	31			
☽	☽	☽	☽			

SEPTEMBER

S	M	T	W	T	F	S
				1	2	3
				☽	☽	☽
4	5	6	7	8	9	10
◗	◗	●	●	●	●	●
11	12	13	14	15	16	17
●	●	●	●	●	◖	◖
18	19	20	21	22	23	24
◖	◖	◖	◖	◖	◖	◖
25	26	27	28	29	30	
○	☽	☽	☽	☽	☽	

OCTOBER

S	M	T	W	T	F	S
30	31					1
☽	☽					☽
2	3	4	5	6	7	8
◗	◗	●	●	●	●	●
9	10	11	12	13	14	15
●	●	●	●	●	◗	◖
16	17	18	19	20	21	22
◖	◖	◖	◖	◖	◖	◖
23	24	25	26	27	28	29
◖	◖	○	☽	☽	☽	☽

NOVEMBER

S	M	T	W	T	F	S
		1	2	3	4	5
		◗	◑	◑	◑	●
6	7	8	9	10	11	12
●	●	●	●	●	●	●
13	14	15	16	17	18	19
●	◖	●	◗	◖	◖	◖
20	21	22	23	24	25	26
◖	◖	◖	○	☽	☽	☽
27	28	29	30			
☽	☽	☽	☽			

DECEMBER

S	M	T	W	T	F	S
				1	2	3
				☽	◑	◑
4	5	6	7	8	9	10
●	●	●	●	●	●	●
11	12	13	14	15	16	17
●	◖	◖	◑	◖	◖	◖
18	19	20	21	22	23	24
◖	◖	◖	◖	◖	○	☽
25	26	27	28	29	30	31
☽	☽	☽	☽	◑	◑	●

○ New moon ● Full moon

January 2022

The sun entered Capricorn, 21 December 2021

The new year begins with a promising aspect: the sun trine Uranus aspect (120 degrees) will ring in something new, unusual or unexpected. If you love surprises you'll love January; if not, consider finding ways to be more adaptable to change!

Luckily, the Capricorn new moon and supermoon on 2 January will help you, and everyone else, to gain a sense of stability this month.

Jupiter in Pisces will add promise and romance to the new year. Jupiter will remain in mystical and inspiring Pisces until early May and will return briefly to Pisces at the end of the year. Jupiter in Pisces will encourage you to approach the year from a philosophical, big-picture humanitarian view, encompassing both an optimistic outlook and one that takes into account the importance of ideals and dreams and a spiritual outlook.

Try to get important paperwork, plans and agreements shipshape before Mercury turns retrograde on 14 January to avoid having to review and revise plans later in the month.

The Cancerian full moon on 17 January may be super intense, so find ways to tune into your emotions during the first half of the month as this will help you to embrace new ideas. You'll be better able to negotiate the challenges or emotional hurdles around the 11th, 17th and 28th as a result.

Adopt a glass-half-full approach to developments in January, as this will enable you to direct your mind to important activities and loved ones rather than being easily distracted by strong emotions and the retrospective, nostalgic mood generated by the Venus retrograde.

For Capricorns

The year begins with a Capricorn new moon, and you'll be happy to turn a corner in a personal endeavour. You may even unexpectedly meet someone special or hear good news on the work or health front in the new year.

The new moon on 2 January points to fresh developments in your daily routine. You may enjoy an extended holiday or must alter your health routine to accommodate developments. Late December–born Capricorns will find this new moon particularly decisive in your personal life as you turn a corner.

The Cancer full moon on 17 January may well be intense as deep emotions well up, either in yourself or someone close. Direct your attention to what and who has main priority in your life to avoid being swept up in events that distract you from your goals.

Be prepared to innovate and to find new ways to communicate with those you love.

Venus retrograde until the end of January will add a nostalgic tone to the month; you may even reunite with someone special and begin where you left off.

INTENTIONS *for the* YEAR

MONDAY 27 DECEMBER

TUESDAY 28

WEDNESDAY 29

THURSDAY 30

FRIDAY 31

SATURDAY 1 〈

Sun trine Uranus: happy New Year! Expect unexpected news and be adaptable to other people's ideas. Moon enters Capricorn late at night.

SUNDAY 2 ○

New moon and supermoon in Capricorn; Mercury semi-sextile Jupiter: a good time for talks and travel and to turn a corner with a favourite project, endeavour or relationship.

		JANUARY				
S	M	T	W	T	F	S
						1
2	3	4	5	6	7	8
9	10	11	12	13	14	15
16	17	18	19	20	21	22
23	24	25	26	27	28	29
30	31					

MONDAY 3 ☽

Moon enters Aquarius.

TUESDAY 4 ☽

Moon in Aquarius.

WEDNESDAY 5 ☽

Venus sextile Neptune: a lovely day for creativity, romance, art and music. Financial decisions may need to be made. Your intuition is likely to be strong, so trust it! Moon in Aquarius.

THURSDAY 6 ☽

Moon in Pisces.

FRIDAY 7 ☽

Moon in Pisces.

SATURDAY 8 ☽

Venus semi-sextile Mars: a good day for get-togethers, romance, the arts and sports. Moon in Aries.

SUNDAY 9 ☽

Sun conjunct Venus: you'll enjoy the company of someone special, so organise a date! Moon in Aries.

			JANUARY			
S	M	T	W	T	F	S
						1
2	3	4	5	6	7	8
9	10	11	12	13	14	15
16	17	18	19	20	21	22
23	24	25	26	27	28	29
30	31					

MONDAY 10

Moon enters Taurus.

TUESDAY 11

Sun sextile Neptune; Mars square Neptune: a lovely get-together will be enjoyable. You may be forgetful or superidealistic, so be careful with key decisions. Moon in Taurus.

WEDNESDAY 12

Moon in Taurus

THURSDAY 13

Moon in Gemini.

FRIDAY 14 ●

Mercury turns retrograde: you may receive key news that merits careful focus. Aim to tie up loose ends of paperwork if possible. Moon in Gemini.

SATURDAY 15 ●

Moon enters Cancer.

SUNDAY 16 ●

Sun conjunct Pluto: you may receive intense news or feel more emotional than usual. Take time out when you can. Moon in Cancer.

			JANUARY			
S	M	T	W	T	F	S
						1
2	3	4	5	6	7	8
9	10	11	12	13	14	15
16	17	18	19	20	21	22
23	24	25	26	27	28	29
30	31					

MONDAY 17 ●

Full moon in Cancer; Venus semi-sextile Saturn: this is a good day to make decisions based on practicalities. You'll enjoy a get-together, and may receive a compliment or positive financial news; however, you may feel more emotional than usual. Trust your intuition; it is strong now.

TUESDAY 18 ●

Moon in Leo.

WEDNESDAY 19 ●

Mars semi-sextile Pluto: a great time to get projects moving and to make changes in important areas of your life. Moon in Leo.

THURSDAY 20 ●

The sun enters Aquarius: you may feel more adventurous and readier to develop your projects. Moon enters Virgo.

FRIDAY 21 ●

Moon in Virgo.

SATURDAY 22 ●

Mercury semi-sextile Jupiter: a good day for meetings, talks and travel plans.
Moon enters Libra.

SUNDAY 23 ◖

Sun conjunct Mercury: a lovely day for get-togethers and for writing and
creativity. You may receive a visit, hear key news or return to an old haunt.
Moon in Libra.

			JANUARY			
S	M	T	W	T	F	S
						1
2	3	4	5	6	7	8
9	10	11	12	13	14	15
16	17	18	19	20	21	22
23	24	25	26	27	28	29
30	31					

January to February 2022

Sun enters Aquarius, 20 January

The next four weeks will be ideal for getting more involved with what and who makes you feel the most fulfilled in life. The end of January is particularly upbeat where meetings, talks and get-togethers are concerned. Take the initiative to get the ball rolling in areas in which you wish to see progress. Just be careful with planning towards the 29th and 30th due to the likelihood of an unexpected change of plan.

Ensure as you progress through February you list your priorities, or you may be prone to being easily misled by other people's ideas and by pie-in-the-sky notions.

The new moon in Aquarius on 1 February is particularly conducive to new ideas and plans, but remember to also be practical and realistic: this new moon is conjunct Saturn, suggesting you be down to earth as opposed to allowing your imagination to run away with you. If developments seem restrictive or limiting it will be a good opportunity to find ways to get more room to move in your own life and to be more innovative moving forward.

The conjunction of the sun and Saturn on 4 February will be ideal for making a commitment such as negotiating a work contract or considering a commitment to someone close. You may find at this time that you go over an old agreement and make changes to it, so this is also a good time for renegotiating existing arrangements.

You'll find many of your projects will gain traction towards the Leo full moon on 16 February.

For Aquarians

The sun in Aquarius makes this your time of year! As Mercury is retrograde until 4 February it's a good time to review and to rethink some of your work and health practices to ensure they still align with your big-picture plans. Once Mercury enters Capricorn on 26 January you may discover some of your work practices seem stuck (or even boring!), but if you can see this phase until 15 February as a good time to tie up loose ends either at work or in your personal life you will emerge all the better for it.

The Aquarian new moon on 1 February will provide insight into how to gain more security in your life. Be adventurous and willing to make changes in your life, otherwise this new moon conjunct Saturn may bring out your stubbornness.

The Leo full moon on 16 February will signal a turning point in your relationships. If a particular relationship has been on the rocks for some time this could be the final act. A serendipitous meeting may open doors to a fresh understanding of someone and, if you're single, you may meet an earthy yet dynamic character so be sure to mingle at this full moon!

MONDAY 24 ◖

Moon in Libra.

TUESDAY 25 ◖

Mercury semi-sextile Mars: a good day to get things done. Aim to boost projects. If you've been feeling under the weather, this is a good day for health and beauty appointments. Moon in Scorpio.

WEDNESDAY 26 ◖

Mercury enters Capricorn: you may revisit important matters that are not yet completely decided upon. Aim to be flexible with your ideas and avoid obstinacy. Moon in Scorpio.

THURSDAY 27 ◖

Moon in Sagittarius.

FRIDAY 28 ☾

Moon in Sagittarius.

SATURDAY 29 ☾

Mercury conjunct Pluto: you may hear intense news that will merit further research. Avoid conversations that get out of control. Aim for balance. Travel plans may need to be rethought. A trip will take you somewhere transformative. Moon in Capricorn.

SUNDAY 30 ☾

Sun square Uranus: you may hear unexpected news or will need to make unforeseen or sudden changes to plans. Be practical for the best results. Moon in Capricorn.

			JANUARY			
S	M	T	W	T	F	S
						1
2	3	4	5	6	7	8
9	10	11	12	13	14	15
16	17	18	19	20	21	22
23	24	25	26	27	28	29
30	31					

MONDAY 31

Sun semi-sextile Venus: a good day for health and beauty appointments. You'll enjoy getting together with someone you love. Moon in Aquarius.

TUESDAY 1

New moon in Aquarius: this is a great time to begin something new and innovative. Be imaginative but also practical and realistic given the prevailing circumstances.

WEDNESDAY 2

Moon enters Pisces.

THURSDAY 3

Moon in Pisces.

FRIDAY 4 .)

*Sun conjunct Saturn; Mercury ends its retrograde phase: this is a good day
to make agreements and commitments, however, you must ensure you are
not limiting your options too much. Consider negotiations today and making
agreements towards mid-month. Moon in Pisces.*

SATURDAY 5)

Moon in Aries.

SUNDAY 6)

Moon in Aries.

		FEBRUARY				
S	M	T	W	T	F	S
		1	2	3	4	5
6	7	8	9	10	11	12
13	14	15	16	17	18	19
20	21	22	23	24	25	26
27	28					

MONDAY 7

Moon in Taurus.

TUESDAY 8

Mars trine Uranus: this is an excellent day to try something new, be it a new work option, venture or activity. You may also enjoy a spontaneous meeting or event. Moon in Taurus.

WEDNESDAY 9

Moon in Gemini.

THURSDAY 10

Sun semi-sextile Neptune: you'll enjoy getting together with like-minded and inspired people. It's a good day for creativity, the arts and romance. Moon in Gemini.

FRIDAY 11 ●

Mercury conjunct Pluto: key discussions could signal important changes to come. Avoid taking someone's opinions personally. You may feel supersensitive, so take things one step at a time. Moon in Cancer.

SATURDAY 12 ●

Moon in Cancer.

SUNDAY 13 ●

Moon in Cancer.

	FEBRUARY					
S	M	T	W	T	F	S
		1	2	3	4	5
6	7	8	9	10	11	12
13	14	15	16	17	18	19
20	21	22	23	24	25	26
27	28					

MONDAY 14 ●

Mercury enters Aquarius; moon's north node trine Pluto: happy St Valentine's Day! Expect out-of-the-ordinary communications and coincidences. Be original and bold! You may hear from an old flame or meet someone significant. Moon in Leo.

TUESDAY 15 ●

Sun square moon's nodes: be open to a new path. Avoid a battle of egos. Moon in Leo.

WEDNESDAY 16 ●

Full moon in Leo; Venus conjunct Mars: you'll enjoy a get-together with someone you love, and key news is likely. If making long-range decisions, ensure these align with your big-picture values and spiritual beliefs. Moon enters Virgo in the evening.

THURSDAY 17 ●

Venus and Mars semi-sextile Saturn; Jupiter sextile Uranus: expect an unexpected development that will require focus. It's a good day for spontaneous meeting and talks and also to make a commitment to a new idea or path. Moon in Virgo.

FRIDAY 18 ●

Sun enters Pisces: an inspiring time awaits but you must be careful to follow your passions and interests to avoid being distracted. Moon in Virgo.

SATURDAY 19 ●

Moon in Libra.

SUNDAY 20 ●

Moon in Libra.

	FEBRUARY					
S	M	T	W	T	F	S
		1	2	3	4	5
6	7	8	9	10	11	12
13	14	15	16	17	18	19
20	21	22	23	24	25	26
27	28					

february to march 2022

Sun enters Pisces, 18 February

There will be no planets retrograde this zodiacal month, suggesting you can make great headway. However, an intense and eventful start to March will bring your focus to events that must be attended to in practical terms. Despite this, there will be many reasons to trust your intuition while at the same time being guided by inspiration and creativity. To ensure you make informed decisions, combine the realities and practicalities of your circumstances with inspired plans.

The Pisces new moon on 2 March provides the opportunity to dream big, even if your options seem to involve dramatic personal transformations or a leap of faith. You'll experience opportunities to move ahead with your various ventures and to find ways to put in place optimistic plans.

This process will be most noticeable around 6 March, when Venus and Mars leave practical and staid Capricorn and enter innovative, adventurous Aquarius. As these two punchy planets will also conjunct at the same time, expect important news and developments that will ask that you look outside the box at your circumstances and come up with a fresh approach.

The main pitfall this Piscean month is to avoid being super idealistic; instead, keep your feet firmly on the ground. The Virgo full moon on 18 March will spotlight the importance of good health, vitality and investment in your own well-being in the most practical yet innovative way possible.

For Pisces

This Pisces season will be particularly transformative for you. If you love change you'll love the upcoming four weeks, especially if you've already put plans in motion for inspiring developments. Just ensure you are as practical as you are positive. The new moon in Pisces on 2 March may bring a surprise your way and will support the development of new ideas, plans and ventures.

The full moon in Virgo on 18 March will indicate if your expectations have been unrealistic. If you find your plans are practical and actionable you'll enjoy the opportunity to bask in the success your careful planning brings. However, if you discover that some of your plans are simply impracticable in the current climate of change you'll realise the importance of being realistic.

Be prepared nevertheless to leave your comfort zone and to innovate. Venus and Mars in Aquarius for the next month will help in this endeavour, and Saturn in Aquarius until early 2023 will help you to be real while following your intuition and ideals.

MONDAY 21 ●

Moon enters Scorpio.

TUESDAY 22 ●

Moon in Scorpio.

WEDNESDAY 23 ●

Mars sextile Neptune: you'll be drawn to romance, the arts and music. You may be super idealistic and forgetful, so ensure you focus more than usual! Moon in Sagittarius.

THURSDAY 24 ◐

Venus sextile Neptune: a lovely day for romance, so make a date! But if you're working, keep an eye on details and avoid forgetfulness and delays. You may be easily influenced, so maintain perspective. Moon in Sagittarius.

FRIDAY 25 ◖

Mercury square Uranus: be prepared to go the extra yards to ensure everyone is on the same page as you or you may experience delays and misunderstandings. Ensure you plan ahead to avoid disappointment. Moon enters Capricorn.

SATURDAY 26 ◖

Mercury semi-sextile Jupiter: communications may be better. It's a good day for a short trip or get-together. Avoid overspending at the shops! Moon in Capricorn.

SUNDAY 27 ◖

Moon enters Aquarius.

		FEBRUARY				
S	M	T	W	T	F	S
		1	2	3	4	5
6	7	8	9	10	11	12
13	14	15	16	17	18	19
20	21	22	23	24	25	26
27	28					

MONDAY 28 (

Moon in Aquarius.

TUESDAY 1 (

Moon enters Pisces.

WEDNESDAY 2 ○

New moon in Pisces; sun sextile Uranus: a good time to consider your dreams and to place your intention to involve more art, romance and creativity in your life. You may be surprised by news. It's a good time to try something new and inspiring. Trust your instincts.

THURSDAY 3)

Venus and Mars conjunct Pluto: this is likely to be an intense day, so ensure you take things one step at a time. Developments could signal considerable change in your life. Moon in Pisces.

FRIDAY 4)

Moon in Aries.

SATURDAY 5)

Sun conjunct Jupiter; Mercury semi-sextile Neptune: matters are likely to be larger than life. You may experience unexpected developments that ask you to be both inspired and practical. Moon in Aries.

SUNDAY 6)

Venus and Mars enter Aquarius; Venus conjunct Mars: a fresh development will ask that you focus on innovative and imaginative ways forward. You may receive unexpected news. Moon in Taurus.

			MARCH			
S	M	T	W	T	F	S
		1	2	3	4	5
6	7	8	9	10	11	12
13	14	15	16	17	18	19
20	21	22	23	24	25	26
27	28	29	30	31		

MONDAY 7   ❯

Moon in Taurus.

TUESDAY 8   ❯

Mercury semi-sextile Pluto: this is a lovely day for making plans for travel and get-togethers and getting ahead with talks and negotiations. Moon enters Gemini.

WEDNESDAY 9   ❯

Moon in Gemini.

THURSDAY 10   ❯

Mercury enters Pisces; sun semi-sextile Saturn: a good day to make an inspired commitment if you've done your research. If you're looking for work, this is a good time to circulate your resume and for interviews. Be optimistic but also practical. Moon in Gemini.

FRIDAY 11

Moon in Cancer.

SATURDAY 12

Moon in Cancer.

SUNDAY 13

Sun conjunct Neptune; Mercury semi-sextile Mars: this is a good day for romance, art and creativity. You'll enjoy relaxing events such as a visit to an art gallery or music and dance. Avoid being super idealistic. Moon enters Leo.

	MARCH					
S	M	T	W	T	F	S
		1	2	3	4	5
6	7	8	9	10	11	12
13	14	15	16	17	18	19
20	21	22	23	24	25	26
27	28	29	30	31		

MONDAY 14   ●

Mercury semi-sextile Venus: a good time for talks and negotiations. Moon in Leo.

TUESDAY 15   ●

Moon in Leo.

WEDNESDAY 16   ●

Moon in Virgo.

THURSDAY 17   ●

Mercury sextile Uranus: be ready for unexpected news or developments and to be adaptable. It's a good day to try something new. Moon in Virgo.

FRIDAY 18 ●

Full moon in Virgo: a good time to improve health, well-being and vitality. You may experience an opportunity to boost your personal life or a venture. Be optimistic and research your options.

SATURDAY 19 ●

Moon in Libra.

SUNDAY 20 ●

Sun enters Aries; spring equinox: this is a period of growth and a good time to promote new plans and ideas. Moon in Scorpio.

			MARCH			
S	M	T	W	T	F	S
		1	2	3	4	5
6	7	8	9	10	11	12
13	14	15	16	17	18	19
20	21	22	23	24	25	26
27	28	29	30	31		

March to
April 2022

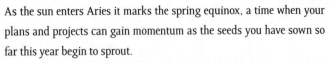

Sun enters Aries, 20 March

As the sun enters Aries it marks the spring equinox, a time when your plans and projects can gain momentum as the seeds you have sown so far this year begin to sprout.

This is another zodiacal month with no planets retrograde, so it's all systems go. If you prefer life to be calmer it's important to take measures to slow things down to avoid feeling under pressure.

The Aries new moon on 1 April will be pivotal regarding health and well-being and your decisions moving forward.

Romance could thrive in early April, so if you've been meaning to ask someone out or wish to reignite passion in your relationship this is it! You may hear from an old flame or reignite a close friendship.

As Venus enters Pisces on 5 April you're likely to be increasingly philosophical, creative and romantic. April is a good month to indulge in your favourite passions and fantasies but avoid allowing your imagination to run away with you, especially when Jupiter conjuncts Neptune on 12 April.

You may be drawn to the past and must be aware you could easily romanticise the past when the present has so much more to offer. Travel and broadening your horizons will appeal, but you must plan carefully to avoid disappointment.

Exaggeration and grandiose plans could lead to mistakes being made, but if you take things one step at a time you could make great progress. Once Mercury enters Taurus on 11 April communications will become more stable and secure, but you must avoid obstinacy at the same time, especially around the Libran full moon on 16 April.

For Aries

Both the sun and Chiron in your sign will be joined by Mercury from 27 March. There will be no planets retrograde, a scenario that makes this month perfect for improving your health and that of others. And the generally go-ahead mood this zodiacal month will certainly suit you.

The new moon in Aries on 1 April will be conjunct Mercury and Chiron, suggesting important health or personal news. You may find this new moon is particularly poignant, especially if it's your birthday.

You'll notice a distinct shift in tempo or mood around 5 April as Venus enters Pisces and your sign's ruler, Mars, conjuncts Saturn. You may discover the perfection inherent in a plan or, alternatively, its limitations. If the latter, you will find imaginative and innovative ways to get ahead.

The Libran full moon on 16 April is a transformative one. If you experience opposition to your plans see this as a way to perfect your ideas. Opportunities can come disguised as obstacles.

MONDAY 21 ●

Mercury conjunct Jupiter in Pisces: important news may require further research. This is a good time to take a trip and for talks. Be spontaneous but avoid snap decisions, especially financially. Moon in Scorpio.

TUESDAY 22 ●

Mercury semi-sextile Saturn; Mars square Uranus: you may experience a surprise or may feel pressured to be more spontaneous. Nevertheless, it's a good day for talks and financial progress and to make fresh agreements. You may enjoy a trip but must avoid impulsiveness. Moon enters Sagittarius.

WEDNESDAY 23 ●

Mercury conjunct Neptune: a good day for spiritual and artistic endeavours; you may also enjoy being in nature. Key news may arrive and you may plan or take a trip. Moon in Sagittarius.

THURSDAY 24 ◖

Moon enters Capricorn.

FRIDAY 25 ◖

Moon in Capricorn.

SATURDAY 26 ◖

Mercury sextile Pluto: trust your instincts, especially if important changes are on the horizon. You may receive key news and will enjoy a lovely get-together. Moon in Capricorn.

SUNDAY 27 ◖

Mercury enters Aries; Venus semi-sextile Jupiter: communications are likely to get busier over the coming weeks. You'll enjoy doing something different. You'll be drawn to romance, love, art, music and good company. Moon in Aquarius.

MARCH

S	M	T	W	T	F	S
		1	2	3	4	5
6	7	8	9	10	11	12
13	14	15	16	17	18	19
20	21	22	23	24	25	26
27	28	29	30	31		

MONDAY 28 (

Venus conjunct Saturn; moon's north node sextile Neptune: a good day for work and business and for money-making and financial decisions. You may gain direction and inspiration and be ready to make a commitment to a project or a special person. Moon in Aquarius.

TUESDAY 29 (

Moon in Pisces.

WEDNESDAY 30 (

Venus semi-sextile Neptune: a good day for art, creativity, dance and romance, however, you may be a little idealistic and have your head in the clouds so avoid being absent-minded. Moon in Pisces.

THURSDAY 31 (

Moon in Aries.

FRIDAY 1 ○

New moon in Aries: this new moon will be conjunct Mercury and Chiron, suggesting important health news is on the way. You may find this new moon is particularly poignant or pivotal for you, especially if it's your birthday.

SATURDAY 2 ☽

Sun conjunct Mercury; sun and Mercury semi-sextile Uranus: expect the unexpected! You'll enjoy an impromptu event. Key decisions can be made now and you may even surprise yourself! Moon enters Taurus.

SUNDAY 3 ☽

Venus semi-sextile Pluto: this is a good day to make changes that could be long term. Romance will thrive under these stars, so organise a date! Moon in Taurus.

| | | APRIL | | | | |
S	M	T	W	T	F	S
					1	2
3	4	5	6	7	8	9
10	11	12	13	14	15	16
17	18	19	20	21	22	23
24	25	26	27	28	29	30

MONDAY 4)

Mars semi-sextile Jupiter: a good time to put clever plans in motion. You may enjoy being more spontaneous, especially in finding time to engage in your favourite activities. Moon in Taurus.

TUESDAY 5)

Venus enters Pisces; Mars conjunct Saturn: a real shift in mood and tempo. You may feel under pressure and yet wish to take your time with key decisions. Avoid being coerced unless you excel under pressure. Art, music and romance will appeal. Moon in Gemini.

WEDNESDAY 6)

Mars semi-sextile Neptune; Jupiter semi-sextile Saturn: a good day to talk or come to agreements and for negotiations. You may feel inspired and spontaneous. Moon in Gemini.

THURSDAY 7)

Mercury sextile Saturn; Mercury semi-sextile Jupiter: a good day for travel plans, talks, meetings and social get-togethers. Moon in Cancer.

FRIDAY 8 ❯

Mercury semi-sextile Neptune: romance could flourish, along with art, music and creativity. You may feel inspired to make changes at home. Moon in Cancer.

SATURDAY 9 ❯

Mercury sextile Mars: a good time to push forward with exciting plans. You may feel more inclined to be adventurous and to plan ahead but must research your options first and trust your intuition. Moon in Cancer.

SUNDAY 10 ❯

Mercury square Pluto: misunderstandings and mix-ups are possible. You or someone close may experience intense emotions or receive tough news, so be prepared to think outside the square. Moon in Leo.

			APRIL			
S	M	T	W	T	F	S
					1	2
3	4	5	6	7	8	9
10	11	12	13	14	15	16
17	18	19	20	21	22	23
24	25	26	27	28	29	30

MONDAY 11

Mercury enters Taurus: you may notice communications begin to settle down, especially after recent days. However, you or someone close may feel stubborn, so maintain perspective and be adaptable where practical. Moon in Leo.

TUESDAY 12

Jupiter conjunct Neptune; moon's nodes square Saturn: a meeting will be significant. You may experience a triumph or a breakthrough, but if you experience a disappointment or a delay be conscientious and base your decisions on creating stability and security. Moon enters Virgo.

WEDNESDAY 13

Sun sextile Saturn; Mars semi-sextile Pluto: you can accomplish a great deal, so make plans to succeed! A good day to make agreements and to be practical and get things done. Moon in Virgo.

THURSDAY 14

Sun semi-sextile Jupiter and Neptune: a great day for romance, the arts, music, dance and love! Make plans to enjoy something special if you haven't already. Moon enters Libra.

FRIDAY 15 ●

Mars enters Pisces: there will be more focus on spirituality, the arts and good health over the coming weeks until the end of May, making this an ideal period to focus on your self-development. Moon in Libra.

SATURDAY 16 ●

Full moon in Libra: a good time to ask how you can change your life to bring more love, romance, creativity, art and music into being. Make a wish: it will surely come true!

SUNDAY 17 ●

Moon in Scorpio.

			APRIL			
S	M	T	W	T	F	S
					1	2
3	4	5	6	7	8	9
10	11	12	13	14	15	16
17	18	19	20	21	22	23
24	25	26	27	28	29	30

MONDAY 18   ●

Sun square Pluto; Mercury sextile Venus; Mercury conjunct Uranus: a good day to make great progress and to initiative plans if you have done your research. However, you may hear unexpected news or will experience an out-of-the-ordinary event. Be prepared and patient if plans change or if someone steals your thunder. Moon in Scorpio.

TUESDAY 19   ●

Moon in Sagittarius.

WEDNESDAY 20   ●

Sun enters Taurus: you will feel more practical about your decision-making. You may be drawn to gardening, baking, self-care, sensuality and luxury. Moon in Sagittarius.

THURSDAY 21   ●

Moon in Capricorn.

FRIDAY 22

Moon in Capricorn.

SATURDAY 23

Mercury conjunct moon's north node: you may hear key news from someone special or hear from an old friend or even an ex. Moon in Aquarius.

SUNDAY 24

Mercury square Saturn; Mercury sextile Neptune: a financial or personal matter deserves careful focus. Adopt an open mind. You may be super idealistic or easily influenced. If someone is obstinate, look for a way ahead without arguments. Moon in Aquarius.

		APRIL				
S	M	T	W	T	F	S
					1	2
3	4	5	6	7	8	9
10	11	12	13	14	15	16
17	18	19	20	21	22	23
24	25	26	27	28	29	30

April to May 2022

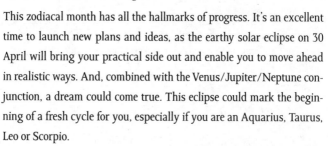

Sun enters Taurus, 20 April

This zodiacal month has all the hallmarks of progress. It's an excellent time to launch new plans and ideas, as the earthy solar eclipse on 30 April will bring your practical side out and enable you to move ahead in realistic ways. And, combined with the Venus/Jupiter/Neptune conjunction, a dream could come true. This eclipse could mark the beginning of a fresh cycle for you, especially if you are an Aquarius, Taurus, Leo or Scorpio.

The first week of May is ideal for communications. Endeavour to get key communications such as major decisions or contracts sorted out before 10 May, when Mercury will turn retrograde for three weeks and communications will not return to their best until mid-June.

The four weeks from 10 May will be ideal for reviewing paperwork, ideas and even relationship decisions if necessary, so this needn't be a time of difficulty or strife if you use it for reflection and reorganisation, especially if you feel you have gone off the path.

Venus in Aries for most of May makes it easier this month to facilitate change, both in your personal life and at work, so ensure you take the initiative. The prevalent Jupiter sextile Pluto aspect is particularly supportive of positive change.

Jupiter enters Aries on 11 May, where it will be until the end of October, bringing a more adventurous, upbeat perspective and enabling action-packed ideas to take flight. However, you must avoid butting heads with someone who can be fiery during this phase.

The total lunar eclipse in Scorpio on 16 May will spotlight what must be done to move forward with your closest relationships, especially where strong feelings emerge.

For Taureans

The upcoming eclipse season falls across your sign, signalling this month is a turning point for you either in a relationship (especially April-born Taureans) or at work (especially May-born Taureans). The first eclipse on 30 April will be particularly powerful for those with birthdays.

The partial solar eclipse on 30 April is a marvellous opportunity to move your life forward in the right direction. Dream big and be prepared to anchor your plans in realistic, practical action and you'll find you can succeed in both personal and work matters.

If you were born at the end of April to early May you will be especially drawn to initiate bold changes in your life. These are likely to go well as long as you avoid a battle of egos and a conflict of interests.

The total lunar eclipse in Scorpio on 16 May will be an intense full moon, especially if it's your birthday. You may need to make decisions based on realities and practicalities rather than on hopes.

MONDAY 25   (

Moon in Pisces.

TUESDAY 26   (

Moon in Pisces.

WEDNESDAY 27   (

Mercury sextile Jupiter; Venus conjunct Neptune: this is a good day for a trip, to meet or talk with people you love and for business meetings. It is also a good day for romance! Moon enters Aries.

THURSDAY 28   (

Mercury trine Pluto: a good time to initiate long-term change or at least to discuss your plans. Moon in Aries.

FRIDAY 29 ☾

Mercury enters Gemini; Pluto turns retrograde: you may feel deeper emotions than usual now but will be better able to express yourself during the upcoming week, so make the most of this communicative phase. Moon in Aries.

SATURDAY 30 ○

Partial solar eclipse in Taurus; Venus conjunct Jupiter: a good time to put practical plans in action. Make a wish but be careful, as it'll come true! Romance could flourish. You may receive a compliment or an ego boost.

SUNDAY 1 ☽

Venus sextile Pluto: a lovely day for romance and for changing any aspect of your home, yourself or your relationship you'd like to improve through careful, considered actions and discussions. Moon in Taurus.

			MAY			
S	M	T	W	T	F	S
1	2	3	4	5	6	7
8	9	10	11	12	13	14
15	16	17	18	19	20	21
22	23	24	25	26	27	28
29	30	31				

MONDAY 2)

Venus enters Aries: a good time to be more adventurous over the coming month with planning and floating ideas. Moon in Gemini.

TUESDAY 3)

Jupiter sextile Pluto: another good day to make changes in areas of your life that need altering. Avoid being zealous and idealistic; be practical and realistic for the best results. Moon in Gemini.

WEDNESDAY 4)

Mars sextile Uranus: a good time to do something different. You may receive unexpected news or will need to be more spontaneous. You'll enjoy an impromptu event. Moon in Gemini.

THURSDAY 5)

Sun conjunct Uranus: expect a surprise. You'll enjoy being spontaneous but must be adaptable, especially if you don't like surprises! Moon in Cancer.

FRIDAY 6　　　　　　　　　　　　　　　　　　　　　　❯

Mercury sextile Venus: a good day for talks, meetings and financial developments. If you're considering a big investment ensure you do adequate research, as you may be inclined to be easily led right now. Moon in Cancer.

SATURDAY 7　　　　　　　　　　　　　　　　　　　　　❯

Sun sextile Mars: this will be a productive weekend. You may be super motivated or will enjoy sports, walks and getting things done. Moon in Leo.

SUNDAY 8　　　　　　　　　　　　　　　　　　　　　　❯

Moon in Leo.

MAY

S	M	T	W	T	F	S
1	2	3	4	5	6	7
8	9	10	11	12	13	14
15	16	17	18	19	20	21
22	23	24	25	26	27	28
29	30	31				

MONDAY 9

Moon enters Virgo late at night.

TUESDAY 10

Mercury turns retrograde: aim to brush up on communication skills over the next three weeks. Moon in Virgo.

WEDNESDAY 11

Jupiter enters Aries: you may experience a more upbeat and optimistic outlook over the coming weeks and months, although current developments may draw on your reserves. Be prepared to step into new and adventurous projects and/ or circumstances. Moon in Virgo.

THURSDAY 12

Moon in Libra.

FRIDAY 13 ●

Sun conjunct moon's north node: you may meet someone special or hear key news. Moon in Libra.

SATURDAY 14 ●

Moon in Scorpio.

SUNDAY 15 ●

Sun square Saturn; sun sextile Neptune; Venus conjunct Chiron: you'll find out if your expectations have been unrealistic and will gain the chance to put things right. You will be drawn to look after yourself or someone close. It's a good day to relax when you can! Moon in Scorpio.

			MAY			
S	M	T	W	T	F	S
1	2	3	4	5	6	7
8	9	10	11	12	13	14
15	16	17	18	19	20	21
22	23	24	25	26	27	28
29	30	31				

MONDAY 16 ●

Total lunar eclipse in Scorpio: this is an intense full moon, as many of your decisions will revolve around people close to you. Aim to be practical and avoid rash decisions. Moon enters Sagittarius during the day.

TUESDAY 17 ●

Saturn semi-sextile Neptune: this is a good day to be practical about developments while also aiming for the best-case outcome. Avoid excesses. Moon in Sagittarius.

WEDNESDAY 18 ●

Mars semi-sextile Saturn; Mars conjunct Neptune: you may feel drawn to strive towards your ideals and you could attain goals, but you must be practical. Romance could blossom. Moon in Capricorn.

THURSDAY 19 ●

Sun trine Pluto: you can make a great deal of progress with your ventures and in your personal life and may enjoy a lovely get-together. Just avoid thorny topics but, if you can't, be prepared to be tactful. Moon in Capricorn.

FRIDAY 20 ●

Mercury sextile Jupiter: a good day for talks, trips and negotiations. You may review your plans or return to an old haunt. You may hear from an old friend. Moon in Aquarius.

SATURDAY 21 ◖

Sun enters Gemini; sun conjunct Mercury: expect to receive important news. If you're travelling the trip will bring you back in touch with old friends or family or could be transformative. Moon in Aquarius.

SUNDAY 22 ◖

Mars sextile Pluto: this is a good time to get ahead with plans that could alter your future situation. Be proactive but avoid impulsive decisions. Romance could flourish. Moon enters Pisces.

| | | MAY | | | | |
S	M	T	W	T	F	S
1	2	3	4	5	6	7
8	9	10	11	12	13	14
15	16	17	18	19	20	21
22	23	24	25	26	27	28
29	30	31				

May to June 2022

Sun enters Gemini, 21 May

The sun's conjunction with Mercury on 21 May brings important news and developments. You may benefit from reviewing some of your plans and schedules and being realistic if news is challenging. You may reunite with an old friend or will revisit an old haunt.

As Mars joins Jupiter, the moon, Chiron and Venus in upbeat Aries on 25 May it signals a dynamo, action-packed week so aim to have your plans up and running by then so you can make the most of this proactive time. However, the tough Venus/Pluto aspect (square) at the end of May could set the cat among the pigeons in what will otherwise be a week of opportunities, so be prepared to work hard.

Once Venus has entered steady Taurus on 28 May you'll experience a more settled phase, even if some matters still need to be approached sensitively. And, while the Gemini new moon on 30 May is generally considered a good time to launch new projects, especially those to do with publishing and writing, discussions in early June will require care and attention.

In June the planets of love and desire, Venus and Mars, will be super influential so watch out: this could be a passionate month and sparks could fly. Ensure they are of the positive variety or you may be surprised by how quickly things can get out of control.

Maintain perspective for the best effect, especially around 11 June. From 13 June Mercury will also be supercharged, so it's likely to be a busy, chatty time. The full moon and supermoon on 14 June will spotlight where in your life you will benefit from adjusting expectations.

For Geminis

Keep an eye on extreme and intense emotions at the end of May. Luckily, the new moon in your sign on 30 May will kick-start a fresh phase for you, especially if you were born at the end of May. You may be particularly drawn to engage in new activities and interests and to boost your career and, once your sign's ruler, Mercury, steps into your sign on 13 June, you'll feel increasingly in your element.

The full moon and supermoon on 14 June will spotlight relationships if you were born before mid-June, and will spotlight work if you were born later in June. Be prepared to make changes that enable you to follow your dreams but, as always, be practical and realistic. A work opportunity may arise and, for some, the chance to commit to a new project or relationship.

MONDAY 23 ☾

Mercury enters Taurus; sun sextile Jupiter: you may enjoy a reunion. You'll appreciate the opportunity to do something you love and to meet favourite people. Moon in Pisces.

TUESDAY 24 ☾

Mercury sextile Mars; Venus sextile Saturn: this is a good day for talks. You could make solid agreements, both in your personal life and work and especially regarding finances. You'll also enjoy socialising. Moon enters Aries late at night.

WEDNESDAY 25 ☾

Mars enters Aries; Mercury trine Pluto: you may hear important news and may need to review or revise a past agreement to bring it up to date. You'll enjoy being spontaneous. Moon in Aries.

THURSDAY 26 ☾

Mercury semi-sextile Venus: a good day for talks, meeting and agreements, especially financially. If you're shopping, avoid overspending! Moon in Aries.

FRIDAY 27 ⟨

Venus square Pluto: keep a check on emotions, as someone — perhaps even you — may feel emotional. Avoid allowing deep or negative emotional responses to interfere with positive relationships. Moon in Taurus.

SATURDAY 28 ⟨

Venus enters Taurus: you'll enjoy indulging in more luxury and sensuality over the upcoming few weeks. You may also be tempted to spend more money! Moon in Taurus.

SUNDAY 29 ⟨

Mars conjunct Jupiter: a good day to get things done and to be proactive, but you may tend to be impulsive so ensure everyone is on the same page before making long-term changes. Moon enters Gemini at night.

			MAY			
S	M	T	W	T	F	S
1	2	3	4	5	6	7
8	9	10	11	12	13	14
15	16	17	18	19	20	21
22	23	24	25	26	27	28
29	30	31				

MONDAY 30 ○

New moon in Gemini: a good time to initiate important plans and to get paperwork shipshape. You may be drawn to plan travel and get-togethers.

TUESDAY 31)

Venus semi-sextile Jupiter; Saturn semi-sextile Neptune: a lovely day for meetings and to get ahead with work projects. You may be drawn to putting new ideas in motion over the next few days. Moon in Gemini.

WEDNESDAY 1)

Moon in Cancer.

THURSDAY 2)

Moon in Cancer.

FRIDAY 3 ❭

Mercury ends its retrograde phase: communications and travel are likely to gradually become easier over the next few weeks. You may receive key news or plan a trip. Moon enters Leo at night.

SATURDAY 4 ❭

Venus semi-sextile Mars: an effective time to set the wheels of various plans in motion. A good time for get-togethers. Moon in Leo.

SUNDAY 5 ❭

Moon in Leo.

		JUNE				
S	M	T	W	T	F	S
			1	2	3	4
5	6	7	8	9	10	11
12	13	14	15	16	17	18
19	20	21	22	23	24	25
26	27	28	29	30		

MONDAY 6 ❭

Moon in Virgo.

TUESDAY 7 ◗

Sun semi-sextile Uranus: expect a surprise. Be adaptable to change, and you'll also enjoy being spontaneous. You may gain direction with a special project, but if it's stuck you'll find ingenious ways to get ahead. Moon in Virgo.

WEDNESDAY 8 ◗

Moon enters Libra.

THURSDAY 9 ●

Moon in Libra.

FRIDAY 10 ●

Mercury trine Pluto: a good day to make changes to your plans and to swiftly get ahead. Emotions may run high, however, so be prepared to slow things down if necessary. Moon enters Scorpio at night.

SATURDAY 11 ●

Venus conjunct Uranus: check your values and principles as you may be surprised by news or a get-together that will be enjoyable for some but intense for others. Avoid impulsiveness, as this could get you into hot water. Moon in Scorpio.

SUNDAY 12 ●

Moon enters Sagittarius late at night.

		JUNE				
S	M	T	W	T	F	S
			1	2	3	4
5	6	7	8	9	10	11
12	13	14	15	16	17	18
19	20	21	22	23	24	25
26	27	28	29	30		

MONDAY 13 ●

Mercury enters Gemini: you'll find communications busy over the coming weeks. Travel plans will gain momentum. Moon in Sagittarius.

TUESDAY 14 ●

Full moon and supermoon in Sagittarius: this full moon may spotlight where in life you have misjudged a situation. Find clarity and aim to set right any areas that need adjustment.

WEDNESDAY 15 ●

Mars conjunct Chiron: avoid accidents and be super careful with words and talks to avoid mix-ups. This is a good time to gain clarity with a health matter. Moon in Capricorn.

THURSDAY 16 ●

Sun trine Saturn; sun square Neptune; Venus conjunct moon's north node: a good time to work methodically towards your goals, especially at work. However, you may be a little forgetful, so ensure you have all the details and facts if making key decisions. You may meet someone important who affects you profoundly. Moon enters Aquarius late at night.

FRIDAY 17

Mars semi-sextile Uranus: a good time to be innovative. You may experience a surprise meeting or receive out-of-the-ordinary news. Moon in Aquarius.

SATURDAY 18

Venus square Saturn: ensure any financial dealings are fair. For some, being careful with negotiations will also apply to your personal life. Moon in Aquarius.

SUNDAY 19

Sun quincunx Pluto; Venus sextile Neptune: a good day for romance, but in business you may tend to be too idealistic. Be practical instead. Moon in Pisces.

			JUNE			
S	M	T	W	T	F	S
			1	2	3	4
5	6	7	8	9	10	11
12	13	14	15	16	17	18
19	20	21	22	23	24	25
26	27	28	29	30		

MONDAY 20 ◖

Moon in Pisces.

TUESDAY 21 ◖

Sun enters Cancer; Venus trine Pluto: summer solstice; as the sun enters Cancer, the summer solstice is a time to bask in high summer and the enjoyment of the harvest soon to come. Romance, the arts, beauty and self-improvement will all appeal. Moon in Aries.

WEDNESDAY 22 ◖

Moon in Aries.

THURSDAY 23 ◖

Moon enters Taurus.

FRIDAY 24 (

Moon in Taurus.

SATURDAY 25 (

Moon in Taurus.

SUNDAY 26 (

Moon in Gemini.

		JUNE				
S	M	T	W	T	F	S
			1	2	3	4
5	6	7	8	9	10	11
12	13	14	15	16	17	18
19	20	21	22	23	24	25
26	27	28	29	30		

June to July 2022

Sun enters Cancer, 21 June

When the sun enters Cancer it marks the northern hemisphere summer solstice. This is the longest day of the year, and we begin to turn our minds to the harvest time arriving soon. It is a time when your activities may peak and you realise the importance of self-nurture and nurturance of others so that you attain your greatest potential.

The trine between Venus and Pluto at the solstice is a positive sign for personal growth and self-development, especially regarding the people you love and the activities and principles you value. This is a good time to take bold strides forward into areas that have true meaning for you, such as important relationships and projects.

The Cancer new moon on 29 June will help you to kick-start bold ventures. However, this will be a time to make sure you have done your groundwork and avoid impulsive decisions, as Mars in Aries until 5 July will create a need to be spontaneous that, when under pressure, could turn to recklessness.

The Capricorn full moon and supermoon on 13 July is a particularly positive full moon as it will shine a light on the most practical and abundant way for you to prioritise the various areas of your life that are most important to you. It is a good time to make a commitment to a particular financial or personal collaboration.

For Cancerians

This will be a particularly progressive month for you, especially if you prioritise those goals and ventures that mean the most to you. The secret to success now lies in being well prepared, so the more research you can do in your various ventures the better will be the outcome. Once Mars is in Taurus from 5 July onwards you are likely to feel all the more capable about your ventures.

The Cancer new moon will kick-start a fresh phase in an important relationship for June Crabs, and July Crabs are likely to begin a fresh daily work or health routine. Be prepared to work methodically towards your goals and you will attain them. The adage 'you make your own luck' applies at this time.

The Capricorn full moon and supermoon on 13 July will be a good time to make a commitment to someone or to a project or idea. Work methodically towards your goals. This is also a good time to boost health, well-being and interests.

MONDAY 27   (

Mercury sextile Chiron; Mars sextile Saturn: be proactive with your projects as your hard work is likely to pay off. You may find merit in re-examining a venture you previously left on the drawing board. A good day for a health or beauty appointment. Moon in Gemini.

TUESDAY 28   (

Sun semi-sextile Venus; Mercury semi-sextile Uranus: expect unexpected news. You may enjoy being spontaneous; a trip could take you somewhere new. You'll enjoy romance, film and the arts, so plan a date! Moon enters Cancer.

WEDNESDAY 29   ○

New moon in Cancer; sun square Jupiter: this new moon is a good time to kick-start adventurous projects that mean a lot to you but only if you have done adequate research, otherwise you risk taking bold steps that are more foolhardy than courageous.

THURSDAY 30   )

Moon in Cancer.

FRIDAY 1)

Moon in Leo.

SATURDAY 2)

Mercury trine Saturn; Mercury square Neptune; Mars square Pluto: this will be an intense day and if you thrive under pressure you'll get things done, but if you prefer peace and calm ensure you take things one step at a time and plan ahead for the best results. Avoid forgetfulness. Moon in Leo.

SUNDAY 3)

Moon enters Virgo.

			JULY			
S	M	T	W	T	F	S
31					1	2
3	4	5	6	7	8	9
10	11	12	13	14	15	16
17	18	19	20	21	22	23
24	25	26	27	28	29	30

MONDAY 4 ❯

Mercury quincunx Pluto: there may be intense undercurrents in some conversations, so avoid stirring up emotions and be practical. Moon in Virgo.

TUESDAY 5 ❯

Mars enters Taurus; Mercury sextile Mars: this is a good day for communications and meetings, so take the initiative. However, you may find some developments are slow moving, so be patient. Moon enters Libra late at night.

WEDNESDAY 6 ❯

Venus sextile Chiron: this is a good day for romance and for improving health and well-being. Moon in Libra.

THURSDAY 7 ❯

Moon in Libra.

FRIDAY 8

Sun square Chiron; Venus semi-sextile Uranus: be prepared to be adaptable but apply the brakes if you feel developments are heading in the wrong direction. You will benefit from looking at an ongoing personal or health matter in a new light. Moon in Scorpio.

SATURDAY 9

Mercury square Jupiter: be careful with communications and travel, as there may be mix-ups and misunderstandings. Moon in Scorpio.

SUNDAY 10

Sun sextile Uranus; Venus semi-sextile moon's north node: expect a surprise or an unforeseen development. Be spontaneous; you may enjoy something different for a change! You may hear from an old friend or family member. Moon enters Sagittarius.

JULY

S	M	T	W	T	F	S
31					1	2
3	4	5	6	7	8	9
10	11	12	13	14	15	16
17	18	19	20	21	22	23
24	25	26	27	28	29	30

MONDAY 11 ●

Moon in Sagittarius.

TUESDAY 12 ●

Moon enters Capricorn.

WEDNESDAY 13 ●

Full moon and supermoon in Capricorn; Venus trine Saturn: a good time to be practical with your projects and to work methodically towards your goals. You may be ready to turn a corner in your work, career or status, finding new meaning in your activities. This is a good day to make agreements.

THURSDAY 14 ●

Venus square Neptune: you may tend to be idealistic, so be inspired but keep abreast of the details and facts as you may be easily misled. Moon enters Aquarius.

FRIDAY 15 ●

Venus quincunx Pluto: this is a good day to feel motivated and to get things done, but some people may find today's developments stressful. Ensure you take things one step at a time. Moon in Aquarius.

SATURDAY 16 ●

Sun conjunct Mercury; sun and Mercury quincunx Saturn: key news, a trip or developments will signal a fresh approach may be necessary at work and/ or with your duties. Take a moment to consider practicalities and be patient! Moon enters Pisces.

SUNDAY 17 ●

Sun and Mercury trine Neptune: a good day for talks, relaxing, romance, the arts and generally for communications. You may be liable to overindulge in good food and wine, so pace yourself! Moon in Pisces.

			JULY			
S	M	T	W	T	F	S
31					1	2
3	4	5	6	7	8	9
10	11	12	13	14	15	16
17	18	19	20	21	22	23
24	25	26	27	28	29	30

MONDAY 18

Mercury opposite Pluto: developments and a meeting could be transformative, even if some news is intense. If you're travelling, your journey could open doors. You may meet someone charming and influential. Moon enters Aries.

TUESDAY 19

Mercury enters Leo: communications are likely to become more outgoing and upbeat and you may feel more sociable over the next two and a half weeks. Moon in Aries.

WEDNESDAY 20

Sun opposite Pluto: a good time to make changes but you must be prepared for intense developments or far-ranging consequences of your actions, so choose your actions wisely. Moon enters Taurus at night.

THURSDAY 21

Moon in Taurus.

FRIDAY 22   ❨

Sun enters Leo: prepare to feel more expressive and to let your inner light shine. If circumstances are tense, take things one step at a time. Moon in Taurus.

SATURDAY 23   ❨

Mercury trine Jupiter: this is a good day for travel, meetings and talks. Just avoid tense topics and aim to find common ground. Moon in Gemini.

SUNDAY 24   ❨

Moon in Gemini.

			JULY			
S	M	T	W	T	F	S
31					1	2
3	4	5	6	7	8	9
10	11	12	13	14	15	16
17	18	19	20	21	22	23
24	25	26	27	28	29	30

July to August 2022

Sun enters Leo, 22 July

As the sun enters Leo it is in opposition to retrograde Pluto, suggesting a degree of internal tension that revolves around where you want to be versus where you are. You may wish to be in a different location or, alternatively, in another space such as feeling you would like to advance at work or in a personal relationship for example. The good news is that this zodiacal month is a great time to make headway towards your chosen destination.

The Leo new moon on 28 July coincides with a lovely conjunction between Mars, Uranus and the moon's north node in Taurus, suggesting important developments that could open doors in unexpected ways. If you're Taurus or Scorpio and single you may unexpectedly meet someone. The sun/Jupiter trine on 31 July could bring good luck your way; however, the alignment between Mars and Uranus could also bring upheaval, so ensure you have prepared a rock-solid foundation for your projects and interests to avoid disappointment.

You'll discover around the full moon in Aquarius on 12 August what needs most attention in your life as particular interests, activities and relationships come under the spotlight. Be prepared to look outside the box at your various options. You may well get the green light on various projects and plans but, if not, check you are well informed and avoid being distracted by what isn't working and focus on what is.

For Leos

The next few weeks could be transformative both at work and health-wise, so ensure you are practical and take steps to make things happen the way you want them to!

There's a truly go-ahead dynamic atmosphere in July and August, but if you feel you are not completely happy with making changes in your life or with escalating projects and circumstances that are already in place there may be wisdom in your approach, as some tough aspects between Uranus, Mars, Venus and Saturn could produce conflict and arguments.

The Leo new moon on 28 July will be a call to action for you to instigate your plans and projects. This is an auspicious new moon for launching new ideas and to begin new ventures, both at work and in your personal life; however, if you experience a surprise or seeming obstacle to your plans then find ways to move ahead innovatively. The key to your success will lie in being resourceful and imaginative. The same applies for the days around the Aquarian full moon on 12 August: the more you can look outside the square at your options the better will be your progress. This will apply predominantly to your personal life and, for mid-August Leos, to work and health.

MONDAY 25 ☽

Venus square Jupiter: this is a good day to gain insight into how someone truly feels about an important matter. Avoid snap decisions. Plan ahead over the next two days to avoid travel delays. Moon enters Cancer in the evening.

TUESDAY 26 ☽

Mercury square Mars: be patient with talks and travel. Avoid impulsiveness. You could accomplish a great deal but must be patient. Moon in Cancer.

WEDNESDAY 27 ☽

Mercury trine Chiron: a good day for health and beauty treatments. It's also a good day to build bridges with someone you have quarrelled with. Moon in Cancer.

THURSDAY 28 ○

New moon in Leo; Mercury square Uranus: expect an unforeseen development or news. This could kick-start a fresh chapter that brings a great deal of change your way, so plan ahead. Avoid rash decisions.

FRIDAY 29)

Moon in Leo.

SATURDAY 30)

Moon enters Virgo.

SUNDAY 31)

Sun trine Jupiter; Mercury opposite Saturn; moon's north node conjunct Uranus: this is a good day to make decisions and a commitment but you must avoid limiting your options too much. Finances can be decided upon. A father figure may have key news. You may unexpectedly meet someone you feel a strong destiny link with. Moon in Virgo.

		JULY				
S	M	T	W	T	F	S
31					1	2
3	4	5	6	7	8	9
10	11	12	13	14	15	16
17	18	19	20	21	22	23
24	25	26	27	28	29	30

MONDAY 1)

Mercury quincunx Neptune; moon's north node conjunct Mars: you may meet someone you feel a fated or strong link with. Meetings may be spontaneous. You must be clear about your goals to avoid disappointment. Moon in Virgo.

TUESDAY 2)

Mars conjunct Uranus; Venus sextile Mars: expect unforeseen developments unless you already experienced a surprise during the last few days. Aim for balance but be prepared to be spontaneous without being reckless. Moon in Libra.

WEDNESDAY 3)

Venus sextile Uranus: you may have an unexpected surprise. Moon in Libra.

THURSDAY 4)

Moon enters Scorpio.

FRIDAY 5

Venus quincunx Saturn: hard work or a financial situation will merit focus. Rest assured you can reach your goals when you focus on a good outcome. Moon in Scorpio.

SATURDAY 6

Moon enters Sagittarius.

SUNDAY 7

Venus trine Neptune; Mars square Saturn: hard work will pay off. Approach a hurdle with the full knowledge you can overcome it. Be positive about love; you may need to pay more attention to it. Moon in Sagittarius.

		AUGUST				
S	M	T	W	T	F	S
	1	2	3	4	5	6
7	8	9	10	11	12	13
14	15	16	17	18	19	20
21	22	23	24	25	26	27
28	29	30	31			

MONDAY 8

Sun trine Chiron: this is a healing day, and you can overcome hurdles with a compassionate and positive approach. It is a good day for health and beauty appointments. Moon enters Capricorn.

TUESDAY 9

Mercury quincunx Jupiter; Venus opposite Pluto: emotions may run high, so take a deep breath and focus on positive outcomes, of which there may be many. Plan ahead to avoid traffic delays. Romance and passion could flourish, but you must avoid arguments. Moon in Capricorn.

WEDNESDAY 10

Moon enters Aquarius.

THURSDAY 11

Venus enters Leo; sun square Uranus; Mars sextile Neptune: you may be surprised by developments and will do well to go with the flow, but you should avoid impulsive moves. Moon in Aquarius.

FRIDAY 12 ●

Full moon in Aquarius: this is a good time to look outside the square at your various options, especially if some matters come to a head or seem stuck. Moon enters Pisces at night.

SATURDAY 13 ●

Moon in Pisces.

SUNDAY 14 ●

Sun opposite Saturn; Mars trine Pluto: this is a good day to come to an agreement or to make a commitment, but you must be sure of your plans and ideas. Avoid making rash decisions and conflict; it could become long-standing. Moon enters Aries at night.

			AUGUST			
S	M	T	W	T	F	S
	1	2	3	4	5	6
7	8	9	10	11	12	13
14	15	16	17	18	19	20
21	22	23	24	25	26	27
28	29	30	31			

MONDAY 15

Mercury trine moon's north node: you may unexpectedly hear from or bump into an old friend. This is a good day for a reunion. Moon in Aries.

TUESDAY 16

Mercury trine Uranus: this is a good day to do something different and to enjoy the company of like-minded people. You may enjoy a spontaneous event but must avoid rash decisions. Moon in Aries.

WEDNESDAY 17

Sun quincunx Neptune: ensure you have all the details if you're making key decisions or you could make mistakes. Avoid being pressured into making decisions. Moon in Taurus.

THURSDAY 18

Venus trine Jupiter; Mercury quincunx Saturn: this is a good day for romance and the arts and enjoying time with someone you love. Just avoid talking at cross purposes; make sure you're on the same page. Moon in Taurus.

FRIDAY 19 ◖

Sun quincunx Pluto: you can make great progress but must avoid power struggles. Moon in Gemini.

SATURDAY 20 ◖

Mars enters Gemini: communications may be busy. Avoid being rushed into decision-making. Moon in Gemini.

SUNDAY 21 ◖

Mercury opposite Neptune: romance and relaxation will be drawcards but you must avoid forgetfulness and absent-mindedness. Avoid misplacing valuables and communication mix-ups. Moon in Gemini.

		AUGUST				
S	M	T	W	T	F	S
	1	2	3	4	5	6
7	8	9	10	11	12	13
14	15	16	17	18	19	20
21	22	23	24	25	26	27
28	29	30	31			

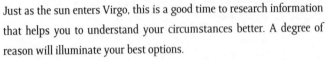

August to September 2022

Sun enters Virgo, 23 August

Just as the sun enters Virgo, this is a good time to research information that helps you to understand your circumstances better. A degree of reason will illuminate your best options.

A lovely aspect between Venus and Chiron on 24 August will encourage healing and relaxing activities such as art, music, dance and romance.

The Virgo new moon on 27 August may well bring tensions to the surface, so it's vital during this zodiacal month to keep your feet on the ground but to be practical at the same time.

The square between Venus and Uranus and between the sun and Mars at the end of August will make this a time of restlessness and, for some, upheaval, so the more you have a contingency plans in place the better it will be for you. You may be drawn to make a commitment to a project, work or an idea, which could work as long as you have been careful with the details.

As Venus joins the sun in Virgo on 5 September you may also be a little analytical about your emotions. Just avoid overanalysing your feelings, as this could bring anxiety to the tension you already feel emotionally.

The lead up to the full moon on 10 September may illuminate where you have been labouring under an illusion. Romance could flourish at the full moon, but you must be certain that your affections are reciprocated if you have recently met someone. Key news at this time may be confusing, but you will reach conclusions about the best way forward. If life is truly confusing at this time you will gain insight towards the end of September.

For Virgos

The Virgo new moon on 27 August may bring tension to the surface, so take things one step at a time this month. Luckily, Mercury in Libra will help to bring a little balance into the mix. At the very least you will be looking to establish balance and harmony.

In the lead up to the Pisces full moon on 10 September old vulnerabilities may re-emerge, so ensure you take things carefully especially if you feel tension in relationships.

Key news at the full moon will shed light on your best way forward, and you will gain deeper insight as the month progresses.

The period from 19 to 20 September will be good for initiating some of your plans, although you may prefer to sound them out first and wait until Mercury is no longer retrograde early in October if good communications are vital to the success of your projects.

MONDAY 22   (

Mercury trine Pluto: a good day to make changes that require you to communicate well. Travel and business could go well, but you must avoid impulsiveness. Moon in Cancer.

TUESDAY 23   (

Sun enters Virgo: it is time to focus on health, well-being, work, nurturance, support and help over the next few weeks. Moon in Cancer.

WEDNESDAY 24   (

Venus trine Chiron: you may feel drawn to help someone or may need help yourself. You may find art, music and romance healing. If your love life has been uncertain you may find more certainty. Look for positive solutions. Moon enters Leo.

THURSDAY 25   (

Moon in Leo.

FRIDAY 26 ⟨

Mercury enters Libra: you'll be drawn to express your romantic, artistic side. You may also be drawn to beautiful places. Moon in Leo.

SATURDAY 27 ○

New moon in Virgo; sun square Mars; Venus square Uranus: this is a good time to consider new ideas that can work in practical terms. You may experience a surprise and may need to review some of your earlier decisions. Be spontaneous but avoid impulsiveness; snap decisions could get you into hot water.

SUNDAY 28 ⟩

Venus opposite Saturn: a good day to be practical, realistic and methodical. It's a good time to be cautious with financial transactions, but if you have all the details you can make a commitment. Moon in Virgo.

		AUGUST				
S	M	T	W	T	F	S
	1	2	3	4	5	6
7	8	9	10	11	12	13
14	15	16	17	18	19	20
21	22	23	24	25	26	27
28	29	30	31			

MONDAY 29   )

Moon enters Libra.

TUESDAY 30   )

Sun quincunx Jupiter: you could achieve a great deal but may need to overcome a challenge first. Moon in Libra.

WEDNESDAY 31   )

Venus quincunx Neptune: you'll be drawn to romantic ideas and being imaginative. If the facts match your expectations you could achieve a great deal. Romance could blossom if both you and your partner are patient and mutually respectful. Moon enters Scorpio.

THURSDAY 1   )

Mars sextile Jupiter: a good day to be active and to get things done. A trip or meeting should go well, but you must avoid pre-empting an outcome. Moon in Scorpio.

FRIDAY 2 ❯

Venus quincunx Pluto: some interactions may be intense. Romance could flourish, but you must avoid conflict. Moon enters Sagittarius.

SATURDAY 3 ◗

Mercury opposite Jupiter; Chiron quincunx moon's south node: a key meeting or news will arise. For some it may bring out sensitivities as vulnerabilities surface. Take time out to heal and boost well-being. Moon in Sagittarius.

SUNDAY 4 ◗

Moon in Sagittarius.

		SEPTEMBER				
S	M	T	W	T	F	S
				1	2	3
4	5	6	7	8	9	10
11	12	13	14	15	16	17
18	19	20	21	22	23	24
25	26	27	28	29	30	

MONDAY 5

Venus enters Virgo: you may begin to feel more inclined to talk about your emotions and to find ways to communicate better over the coming weeks. Avoid overanalysing emotions. Moon in Capricorn.

TUESDAY 6

Moon in Capricorn.

WEDNESDAY 7

Moon in Aquarius.

THURSDAY 8

Sun quincunx Chiron: a health or personal matter will deserve careful focus, but you will overcome difficulties as a result. Moon in Aquarius.

FRIDAY 9 ●

Venus quincunx Jupiter: avoid exaggerating emotions and feelings. If challenges arise, take things carefully and you will succeed. Moon in Pisces.

SATURDAY 10 ●

Full moon in Pisces; Mercury turns retrograde: this full moon will spotlight romance, music, the arts, idealism and your beliefs. You may tend to see the world through rose-coloured glasses, so if you're making key decisions ensure you have the facts. You may receive key news.

SUNDAY 11 ●

Sun trine Uranus: you may experience a surprise. It's a good day to take the initiative and to get things done. You'll be drawn to doing something different for a change. Moon in Aries.

SEPTEMBER

S	M	T	W	T	F	S
				1	2	3
4	5	6	7	8	9	10
11	12	13	14	15	16	17
18	19	20	21	22	23	24
25	26	27	28	29	30	

MONDAY 12

Sun quincunx Saturn; Mercury semi-sextile Venus: if you're careful, communications and work will go well. If challenges arise, face them head on and you will overcome the odds. Moon in Aries.

TUESDAY 13

Moon enters Taurus.

WEDNESDAY 14

Moon in Taurus.

THURSDAY 15

Moon enters Gemini at night.

FRIDAY 16 ◗

Sun opposite Neptune; Venus square Mars: mistakes could be made, especially in the love stakes, so before you make major decisions ensure you have the facts straight. This aside, romance could be tense – but that's when passion could ignite! Moon in Gemini.

SATURDAY 17 ◗

Moon in Gemini.

SUNDAY 18 ◗

Mercury opposite Jupiter: you may review information or circumstances that occurred earlier in the month or at the full moon. You may revisit an old haunt or reconnect with someone. Moon enters Cancer.

		SEPTEMBER				
S	M	T	W	T	F	S
				1	2	3
4	5	6	7	8	9	10
11	12	13	14	15	16	17
18	19	20	21	22	23	24
25	26	27	28	29	30	

MONDAY 19 ☾

Sun trine Pluto: considerable developments will mean a significant change. If you'd like to initiate change, this is a positive time to test the water. Moon in Cancer.

TUESDAY 20 ☾

Venus quincunx Saturn; Venus trine Uranus: this is a good time to take the initiative with your plans and projects; you may be surprised. Rise to challenges and be prepared for change or to be spontaneous. Moon enters Leo at night.

WEDNESDAY 21 ☾

Moon in Leo.

THURSDAY 22 ☾

Moon in Leo.

FRIDAY 23 ⟨

Sun enters Libra; Mercury enters Virgo; sun conjunct Mercury: this is the autumn equinox, a time to integrate ideas, give thanks and prepare for winter. Look for balance and a fair go over the coming weeks. Avoid arguments and delays by planning ahead and being patient. Key news arrives. You may enjoy a trip to an old haunt or a visit. Moon in Virgo.

SATURDAY 24 ⟨

Venus opposite Neptune: a lovely day for romance, the arts, music and dance, but if you're unsure of someone or of a project it's important you get the heads-up if possible without overanalysing the situation. Moon in Virgo.

SUNDAY 25 ○

New moon in Libra: this is a transformational new moon. Make a wish but be careful what you wish for: it'll surely come true!

SEPTEMBER

S	M	T	W	T	F	S
				1	2	3
4	5	6	7	8	9	10
11	12	13	14	15	16	17
18	19	20	21	22	23	24
25	26	27	28	29	30	

september to october 2022

Sun enters Libra, 23 September

As the sun enters Libra this is the autumn equinox. And, as the seasons change, this is a good time to seek more harmony and balance in your home life as you'll be spending more time indoors.

Mercury retrograde will step back into Virgo, bringing the need to be analytical and methodical about your aims and goals.

You can make great progress this month and make changes to the way you approach your life and others, but you will need to ensure you have all the required information at your fingertips to avoid over- or underestimating circumstances.

The new moon in Libra on 25 September will bring those areas of your life in which you want to see more balance into sharp focus. Look at what could be done better and find the time to celebrate what works wonderfully already.

Developments in early October will require you to maintain perspective, especially regarding health and well-being in early October and at the Aries full moon on 9 October. Be proactive about making positive change in your life.

The grand trine between the sun, Saturn and Mars suggests that you adopt a philosophical and analytical approach to developments rather than allow emotions to rule. You will need to be spontaneous yet plan ahead well at the same time, making adaptability and multi-tasking qualities to embrace this month. You'll find this easier when Mercury is once more in a strong position and in Libra in mid-October.

For Librans

This is a transformative time for you, so it's wise to take things one step at a time. You may enjoy a super-romantic time but may also be prone to being easily misled or to make an error of judgement.

You'll appreciate the generally go-ahead atmosphere of the last week in September and first week of October, and you'll find out after this time whether your decisions and projects have taken you on the right track.

The Libran new moon on 25 September is an excellent time to redefine some of your goals, especially those to do with a business or personal partner. Changes at work, in your daily routine or at home will be pleasing, but strategy and planning are the keys to success. You could make great progress with a creative or family project but must be prepared to adapt to new circumstances.

The full moon in Aries on 9 October will bring key news: for some health-wise and for others to do with work and changes you wish to see there.

The grand trine between Venus, Mars, the sun and Saturn in mid-October will be an excellent time for planning and taking projects forward. Keep an eye on shifting targets, however, and be prepared to be flexible about decisions. Avoid a confrontational approach as plans and ideas are likely to constantly change.

MONDAY 26)

Sun opposite Jupiter; Mercury conjunct Venus; Venus trine Pluto: this is a good time to make changes in your life, but talks and developments may be intense so take things one step at a time. This may be a lucky day. Moon in Libra.

TUESDAY 27)

Mercury trine Pluto: a good day to discuss your ideas and for meetings. You may wish to return to an old haunt. A trip could be transformative. Moon in Libra.

WEDENSDAY 28)

Mars trine Saturn: a good day to take the initiative, especially at work. Moon in Scorpio.

THURSDAY 29)

Moon in Scorpio.

FRIDAY 30 ⟩

Moon in Sagittarius.

SATURDAY 1 ⟩

Venus opposite Jupiter: this is a good time to reconnect with someone special and to reconsider if any of your projects could advance better. Organising a trip or a long-term venture may appeal. Moon in Sagittarius.

SUNDAY 2 ◗

Mercury ends its retrograde phase: key news may arrive. Communications may improve over the coming weeks. Moon in Capricorn.

			OCTOBER			
S	M	T	W	T	F	S
						1
2	3	4	5	6	7	8
9	10	11	12	13	14	15
16	17	18	19	20	21	22
23	24	25	26	27	28	29
30	31					

MONDAY 3 ◗

Moon in Capricorn.

TUESDAY 4 ◗

Moon enters Aquarius.

WEDNESDAY 5 ●

Moon in Aquarius.

THURSDAY 6 ●

Moon enters Pisces.

FRIDAY 7   ●

*Sun opposite Chiron; sun quincunx moon's north node; Mercury trine
Pluto: key meetings and news may lead to great change. If you experience a
challenge, follow your instincts and you will overcome obstacles. Avoid taking
developments personally by maintaining perspective. A health situation may
require more focus. Moon in Pisces.*

SATURDAY 8   ●

Moon enters Aries.

SUNDAY 9   ●

*Full moon in Aries: this full moon will spotlight your desires and also your
vulnerabilities. Aim to count your blessings as opposed to viewing only what is
not working. This is a good time to boost health and to focus on your well-being
and that of someone close.*

| | | OCTOBER | | | | |
S	M	T	W	T	F	S
						1
2	3	4	5	6	7	8
9	10	11	12	13	14	15
16	17	18	19	20	21	22
23	24	25	26	27	28	29
30	31					

MONDAY 10 ●

Venus opposite Chiron: a good day to boost health and well-being and your appearance. Moon enters Taurus at night.

TUESDAY 11 ●

Mercury enters Libra; sun trine Saturn; sun quincunx Uranus: this is a good time to rethink some of your plans so they are more practical and balanced and easier to implement. Be adaptable. Moon in Taurus.

WEDNESDAY 12 ●

Mercury opposite Jupiter; Mars square Neptune: ensure you have all the details at your fingertips if you are making far-reaching decisions, as mistakes and miscommunications could occur. Be practical and avoid making assumptions. Travel could be delayed, so plan ahead. Moon in Taurus.

THURSDAY 13 ●

Venus quincunx Uranus: be prepared to be flexible and adaptable. Someone may behave unpredictably and your schedule may change unexpectedly. Moon in Gemini.

FRIDAY 14

Venus trine Saturn: this is a good day for making agreements and for enjoying time with someone you love. You may be ready to make a commitment. Moon in Gemini.

SATURDAY 15

Moon enters Cancer.

SUNDAY 16

Sun quincunx Neptune: you'll be inspired by romance, art and music, but if you are making key decisions you must focus on the details and avoid being sidetracked. Moon in Cancer.

| | | OCTOBER | | | | |
S	M	T	W	T	F	S
						1
2	3	4	5	6	7	8
9	10	11	12	13	14	15
16	17	18	19	20	21	22
23	24	25	26	27	28	29
30	31					

MONDAY 17 ◖

Sun trine Mars; Venus quincunx Neptune: you could get a great deal done at work and romance could flourish, but you must avoid being easily influenced and making snap decisions. Moon in Cancer.

TUESDAY 18 ◖

Moon in Leo.

WEDNESDAY 19 ◖

Sun square Pluto; Venus trine Mars: a lovely time for romance and for progressing with projects and initiatives. However, if you feel opposed or events become intense, avoid conflict as it could become long-standing. Find ways to de-escalate tension instead. Moon in Leo.

THURSDAY 20 ◖

Venus square Pluto: this may be another intense day, so find ways to de-stress and unwind when you can. Moon enters Virgo at night.

FRIDAY 21 ☽

Moon in Virgo.

SATURDAY 22 ☽

*Sun conjunct Venus; Mercury quincunx Uranus: this is a good day
for meetings, romance, art and creativity, although there may be a
misunderstanding or unexpected development to contend with. Moon in Virgo.*

SUNDAY 23 ☽

*Sun enters Scorpio; Mercury trine Saturn; sun and Venus quincunx Jupiter:
a more passionate phase begins. This is a good day for talks and to make a
commitment, although someone may surprise you. Moon in Libra.*

| | | OCTOBER | | | | |
S	M	T	W	T	F	S
						1
2	3	4	5	6	7	8
9	10	11	12	13	14	15
16	17	18	19	20	21	22
23	24	25	26	27	28	29
30	31					

october to november 2022

Sun enters Scorpio, 23 October

As the sun enters passionate Scorpio so does amorous Venus, making a conjunction. At the same time, Mercury will trine Saturn, bringing excellent conditions for talks, meetings and agreements. You may even find this a good time to make a commitment to a plan or even to a person!

The Scorpio new moon and partial solar eclipse on 25 October will be a passionate, romantic new moon, ideal for turning a corner in a partnership or marriage. Singles may meet someone new or be drawn to an ex at this time. As always, choose wisely.

There is a retrospective, nostalgic and wistful quality about the beginning of November, as a meeting with an old friend or even partner could bring unexpected developments your way. If you enjoy a challenge in life you'll find early November revitalising, but if you prefer life on an even keel this could be a challenging time for you so ensure you avoid making snap decisions you later come to regret.

This could be an intense time in the lead up to the total lunar eclipse in Taurus on 8 November.

Both Mercury and Venus in Sagittarius from mid-November will put the focus on broadening your horizons, which could be in many different ways: through study, for example, travel or learning new relationship dynamics. Research your options and avoid making decisions based on supposition alone.

For Scorpios

The partial solar eclipse in your sign will be conjunct Venus on 25 October, suggesting you are ready to make a fresh commitment to someone special. If you are single you may meet someone new on this day, so ensure you make plans to socialise. However, if you feel your existing relationship has been on the rocks the upcoming eclipse season could signal a parting of ways. It will be for you to re-evaluate who and what is most important in your life now as you could make great changes.

This will be an intense time but also one where much change can occur. The total lunar eclipse on 8 November will spotlight your true feelings and those of someone close. If you are intent on rekindling or allowing love to blossom, the weekend of 12 November and during the week of 15 November will be a time when you could see love flourish in your life – unless, that is, you have misjudged circumstances. In this case you could experience a serious letdown, so check the reality of your circumstances before you make big changes.

Financial decisions in mid-November will deserve careful appraisal.

MONDAY 24 ◔

Chiron quincunx moon's south node: you may need to get through a difficult conundrum, but rest assured you will. Moon in Libra.

TUESDAY 25 ○

Partial solar eclipse in Scorpio; Mercury quincunx Neptune: this is an excellent time to consider how you could do things better to transform an area of your life where change is long overdue. Keep an eye on communications, as they may be a little confusing or you may be forgetful. Plan ahead to avoid travel delays.

WEDNESDAY 26 ☽

Moon in Scorpio.

THURSDAY 27 ☽

Mercury trine Mars; Mercury square Pluto: this is a good time to be proactive with your ventures and to be more outgoing. However, some circumstances may be intense, so avoid overanalysing situations as you may invite in drama or intrigue. Moon enters Sagittarius.

FRIDAY 28 ☽

Jupiter retrograde enters Pisces: you may be a little nostalgic over the coming weeks but will find this a good time to review some of your plans and ideas. Moon in Sagittarius.

SATURDAY 29 ☽

Mercury enters Scorpio; Mercury quincunx Jupiter: you may feel idealistic, whereas a practical mindset will overcome difficulties. Moon enters Capricorn.

SUNDAY 30 ☽

Moon in Capricorn.

OCTOBER

S	M	T	W	T	F	S
						1
2	3	4	5	6	7	8
9	10	11	12	13	14	15
16	17	18	19	20	21	22
23	24	25	26	27	28	29
30	31					

MONDAY 31

Happy Hallowe'en! This is always a quirky day, and with the moon in Aquarius this evening you're likely to experience a few unexpected surprises. Moon enters Aquarius.

TUESDAY 1

Moon in Aquarius.

WEDNESDAY 2

Venus quincunx Chiron: this could be a time when conversations are intense or challenging, so ensure you are practical. Moon enters Pisces.

THURSDAY 3

Venus conjunct moon's south node: you may go over old ground, meet an old friend or rekindle a relationship. Moon in Pisces.

FRIDAY 4 ●

Moon enters Aries just before midnight GMT.

SATURDAY 5 ●

Sun conjunct moon's south node; sun quincunx Chiron; Venus opposite Uranus: you may feel under pressure due to several meetings or news from someone from your past. Take things one step at a time and avoid snap decisions, although you may need to be spontaneous and embrace change. Moon in Aries.

SUNDAY 6 ●

Mercury conjunct moon's south node: you may hear unexpectedly from someone from your past. Moon in Aries.

		NOVEMBER				
S	M	T	W	T	F	S
		1	2	3	4	5
6	7	8	9	10	11	12
13	14	15	16	17	18	19
20	21	22	23	24	25	26
27	28	29	30			

MONDAY 7 ●

Venus square Saturn: you'll need to negotiate and come to terms with a new arrangement. Some may return to an old haunt. Moon in Taurus.

TUESDAY 8 ●

Total lunar eclipse in Taurus; sun conjunct Mercury: expect the unexpected during this eclipse and its after-effects as key news, travel plans or a meeting take place. You may need to be spontaneous, not stubborn, and must avoid knee-jerk reactions.

WEDNESDAY 9 ●

Sun and Mercury opposite Uranus: expect changes to manifest; the more adaptable you are the better. Luckily, the Gemini moon will help you to be flexible. Moon enters Gemini.

THURSDAY 10 ●

Mercury square Saturn; Venus trine Neptune: communications may be tense, so avoid arguments and find common ground instead. Look for mutually beneficial outcomes. This is a good day for the arts and romance, but you must avoid focusing on what is not working and focus instead on what is working. Moon in Gemini.

FRIDAY 11 ●

Sun square Saturn; Venus quincunx Mars: find the time to look for a practical path ahead; avoid being stubborn or contrary. Moon in Gemini.

SATURDAY 12 ●

Mercury trine Neptune: you or someone else may be particularly persuasive. Avoid forgetfulness and being easily influenced. Romance could flourish, so plan a date or a night in! Moon in Cancer.

SUNDAY 13 ●

Mercury quincunx Mars; Venus sextile Pluto: this could be a passionate day but you must avoid focusing on your differences. Be patient and you could kindle love. Moon in Cancer.

		NOVEMBER				
S	M	T	W	T	F	S
		1	2	3	4	5
6	7	8	9	10	11	12
13	14	15	16	17	18	19
20	21	22	23	24	25	26
27	28	29	30			

MONDAY 14

Moon enters Leo.

TUESDAY 15

Sun trine Neptune; Mercury sextile Pluto; Venus trine Jupiter: this is a good day for talks and to ensure you are on the right track with someone special. Romance, the arts, music and creativity could flourish. Moon in Leo.

WEDNESDAY 16

Venus enters Sagittarius; sun quincunx Mars; Mercury trine Jupiter: when you embrace a project you could make rapid progress despite challenges. There may be travel news. Take things one step at a time to avoid rash decisions. Moon in Leo.

THURSDAY 17

Mercury enters Sagittarius: travel and communications will take increasing focus over the coming weeks. You may feel super drawn to expand your horizons. Moon in Virgo.

FRIDAY 18 ◖

Sun sextile Pluto: this is a good day for making changes where you feel they are necessary. Moon in Virgo.

SATURDAY 19 ◖

Mars square Neptune: ensure you have all the facts straight, especially if making key decisions. Avoid forgetfulness, being easily led and impulsiveness. Moon enters Libra.

SUNDAY 20 ◖

Moon in Libra.

	NOVEMBER					
S	M	T	W	T	F	S
		1	2	3	4	5
6	7	8	9	10	11	12
13	14	15	16	17	18	19
20	21	22	23	24	25	26
27	28	29	30			

MONDAY 21   (

Sun trine Jupiter; Mercury conjunct Venus: you are likely to be optimistic and positive. Key news or a meeting could be decisive. You may also be lucky or will embark on a journey. Moon enters Scorpio in the evening.

TUESDAY 22   (

Sun enters Sagittarius: let your inner adventurer out over the coming weeks. Moon in Scorpio.

WEDNESDAY 23   ○

New moon in Sagittarius: it's time to turn a corner in an adventurous way. Be positive.

THURSDAY 24   )

Moon in Sagittarius.

FRIDAY 25)

Mercury trine Chiron: this is a therapeutic time when health and well-being will be focuses. You may choose to focus on appearance, making this a good time for beauty treatments. Moon enters Capricorn at night.

SATURDAY 26)

Venus trine Chiron: a good day to improve your appearance and well-being. Love could blossom. If you feel super sensitive avoid taking the behaviour of others personally. Meetings could be significant. Moon in Capricorn.

SUNDAY 27)

Mercury quincunx Uranus: expect unforeseen news or an impromptu meeting. Avoid misunderstandings and mix-ups. Moon enters Aquarius at night.

			NOVEMBER			
S	M	T	W	T	F	S
		1	2	3	4	5
6	7	8	9	10	11	12
13	14	15	16	17	18	19
20	21	22	23	24	25	26
27	28	29	30			

November to December 2022

Sun enters Sagittarius, 22 November

The sun, Mercury and Venus in Sagittarius will produce an upbeat feeling at the end of November and will also contribute to a need to expand your horizons. You may be drawn to study, new ideas and ventures or even to travel.

The Sagittarian new moon on 23 November will feel progressive, as fresh horizons beckon. Aim to focus in on the healing and therapeutic qualities of new ventures and circumstances as opposed to the difficulties. Avoid stubbornness and be flexible.

Meetings towards the end of November are likely to be more significant than initially meets the eye and could also be therapeutic or involve the chance to boost health.

A little confusion early in December is best dispelled with research and fact finding. Impulsiveness is best avoided, especially on 9 December when you may be inclined to throw caution to the wind. That said, you'll enjoy being spontaneous and free spirited over these four weeks, and travel and generally embracing fun activities will appeal.

Aim to improve your listening skills in December, as better communication abilities will put you in a stronger position.

For Sagittarians

The sun, Mercury and Venus in your sign point to a busy and eventful time. The new moon in your own sign on 23 November will be refreshing, especially in your daily life, work and health. If any of these areas have been stuck or lacklustre this new moon could help you take adventurous steps into something new, so be inspired and proactive.

There may be a little confusion at the start of December and someone may need your help. If you need some support yourself, be prepared to ask for it. Once Mercury enters practical Capricorn on 6 December you're likely to feel more grounded and capable.

The full moon in Gemini on 8 December may bring to the surface strong emotions or simply a wish to be free. Avoid impulsiveness and look for clever ways to move ahead. Be practical for the best results, or this full moon could spotlight reckless behaviour.

MONDAY 28

Mars trine Saturn: a good day to get things done. You could make a beneficial agreement. Moon in Aquarius.

TUESDAY 29

Mercury opposite Mars; Venus quincunx Uranus: you may receive an out-of-the-ordinary offer. Someone may behave unpredictably, but avoid taking their behaviour personally. Moon in Aquarius.

WEDNESDAY 30

Mercury sextile Saturn: this is a good day for talks and meetings, especially if you have all the facts at your fingertips. Moon in Pisces.

THURSDAY 1

Venus opposite Mars: this is a good time for meetings, although you must ensure you have the facts or your information may be challenged. Avoid conflict and look for common ground. Romance could flourish. Moon in Pisces.

FRIDAY 2 ●

Mercury square Neptune; Venus sextile Saturn: keep an eye on communications as you could make great progress, especially at work and with health matters, but there may be misunderstandings. Avoid impulsiveness; do your research. Plan ahead to avoid travel delays. Moon in Aries.

SATURDAY 3 ●

Sun trine Chiron: there is a therapeutic atmosphere to the weekend. You may be asked to help someone or may need some advice or support yourself. Moon in Aries.

SUNDAY 4 ●

Mercury semi-sextile Pluto; Venus square Neptune: you'll enjoy a get-together but must be prepared to go the extra mile to help or understand someone as their behaviour may be confusing or even mystifying. Moon enters Taurus.

DECEMBER

S	M	T	W	T	F	S
				1	2	3
4	5	6	7	8	9	10
11	12	13	14	15	16	17
18	19	20	21	22	23	24
25	26	27	28	29	30	31

MONDAY 5   ●

Moon in Taurus.

TUESDAY 6   ●

Mercury enters Capricorn; Mercury square Jupiter: you may find communications or travel are delayed or difficult, so ensure you plan ahead and stick to a tried-and-trusted strategy. Avoid misunderstandings. Moon enters Gemini.

WEDNESDAY 7   ●

Sun quincunx Uranus; Venus semi-sextile Pluto: an innovative approach to circumstances will be useful. Be adaptable. Moon in Gemini.

THURSDAY 8   ●

Full moon in Gemini; sun opposite Mars: you can get a great deal done but must avoid impulsiveness and making snap decisions. Moon in Gemini.

FRIDAY 9

●

Mars semi-sextile Uranus: you may feel spontaneous and will enjoy an impromptu get-together. Moon in Cancer.

SATURDAY 10

●

Venus square Jupiter: communications will merit a little care and attention to avoid making already tense situations worse. Aim to listen to someone else's opinion even if you do not agree with it. Moon in Cancer.

SUNDAY 11

●

Venus enters Capricorn: you'll feel more grounded and practical about some of your plans but must avoid stubbornness, both in yourself and others. Moon enters Leo at night.

DECEMBER

S	M	T	W	T	F	S
				1	2	3
4	5	6	7	8	9	10
11	12	13	14	15	16	17
18	19	20	21	22	23	24
25	26	27	28	29	30	31

MONDAY 12

Sun sextile Saturn: this is a good day to be proactive with your projects and make practical plans for exciting ventures. Moon in Leo.

TUESDAY 13

Moon in Leo.

WEDNESDAY 14

Sun square Neptune: aim to be super clear with your interactions or confusion could arise. Take extra time to listen to others. Moon enters Virgo.

THURSDAY 15

Moon in Virgo.

FRIDAY 16 ◗

Mercury quincunx Mars: keep communications straightforward to avoid mix-ups. A challenge can be overcome with attention to detail and flexibility. Moon enters Libra at night.

SATURDAY 17 ◗

Mercury trine Uranus: a change of pace or of place will be enjoyable. You'll appreciate the chance to be spontaneous. Moon in Libra.

SUNDAY 18 ◗

Venus square Chiron: you'll appreciate the opportunity to enjoy the company of like-minded people or someone you love. You may enjoy a beauty or health boost. Romance could blossom but you must avoid misunderstandings. Moon in Libra.

DECEMBER

S	M	T	W	T	F	S
				1	2	3
4	5	6	7	8	9	10
11	12	13	14	15	16	17
18	19	20	21	22	23	24
25	26	27	28	29	30	31

MONDAY 19 ☾

Sun semi-sextile Pluto; Venus quincunx Mars: a good day to make changes and to get together with old friends. Just avoid tenses topics. Moon in Scorpio.

TUESDAY 20 ☾

Moon in Scorpio.

WEDNESDAY 21 ☾

Sun enters Capricorn; sun square Jupiter: collectively, thoughts may turn to the practicalities of the holiday season and to the new year of 2023. Avoid looking only at the obstacles and find ways to enjoy common ground. Avoid travel delays by planning ahead. Moon in Sagittarius.

THURSDAY 22 ☾

Venus trine Uranus: you'll enjoy doing something new and being spontaneous. A lovely get-together will be enjoyable. Moon in Sagittarius.

FRIDAY 23 ○

New moon and supermoon in Capricorn; Mercury semi-sextile Saturn: a good time for get-togethers and to consider in realistic terms how best to make solid plans for a peaceful time.

SATURDAY 24 ☽

Mercury sextile Neptune: a lovely time for romance, get-togethers and creativity. Moon in Capricorn.

SUNDAY 25 ☽

Merry Christmas! Moon in Aquarius.

		DECEMBER				
S	M	T	W	T	F	S
					1	2	3
4	5	6	7	8	9	10
11	12	13	14	15	16	17
18	19	20	21	22	23	24
25	26	27	28	29	30	31

december 2022

Sun enters Capricorn, 21 December

As the sun steps into Capricorn it marks the northern hemisphere winter solstice, a time when we collectively reflect on the hard work we have done all year and prepare to plant new seeds of hope for the coming year.

The mood over Christmas is likely to be more relaxed or harmonious than it was in previous years. You may also enjoy being more spontaneous or doing something different this Christmas and during the lead up to Christmas Day. The new moon on 23 December will be a supermoon, suggesting anything new you put into action at this time will have more significance over time than may at first be apparent.

Christmas Eve has a particularly romantic quality about it, so why not organise a treat?

The new year is likely to bring a little more intensity or tension, so ensure you enjoy a few days off at Christmas and plan to enjoy hassle-free new year festivities.

For more about Capricorn in January 2023 reserve your copy of the *2023 Astrology Diary*; see Rockpool Publishing's website at www.rockpoolpublishing.com.au or www.patsybennett.com.

Wishing everyone a very happy solstice and Yuletide and a happy New Year!

For Capricorns

Just as the sun enters your sign it comes into a tense angle with upbeat Jupiter, suggesting some aspects of your circumstances may not please you at the moment. The good news is that you'll get the chance to make changes and be proactive about setting in motion better circumstances for yourself.

The new moon and supermoon in your sign on 23 December will encourage you to be positive about your prospects and inject fresh optimism into your outlook.

The period just before Christmas is likely to be less stressful than it was in previous years, but once Mercury turns retrograde on 29 December you may need to focus a little more on finances and relationships to ensure the new year is smooth sailing, especially if it's your birthday at the end of December or in early January. When you are careful you'll enjoy your new year all the more!

MONDAY 26)

Moon in Aquarius.

TUESDAY 27)

Venus semi-sextile Saturn: a good day for get-togethers. You're likely to enjoy some retail therapy. Moon in Pisces.

WEDNESDAY 28)

Venus sextile Neptune: a good day for meetings, talks and romance. Moon in Pisces.

THURSDAY 29 ▶

Mercury turns retrograde; Mercury conjunct Venus: this is a chatty day as news arrives. A trip to an old haunt and a financial situation will deserve focus. It's a good time to avoid overspending and to put a fresh budget in place. Moon in Aries.

FRIDAY 30 ●

Sun quincunx Mars: avoid being impulsive, as you may regret rash decisions. If obstacles arise rest assured you can overcome them. Moon in Aries.

SATURDAY 31 ●

Happy New Year! Moon enters Taurus at night.

SUNDAY JANUARY 1 ●

Happy New Year!

		DECEMBER				
S	M	T	W	T	F	S
				1	2	3
4	5	6	7	8	9	10
11	12	13	14	15	16	17
18	19	20	21	22	23	24
25	26	27	28	29	30	31

NOTES

NOTES

NOTES

NOTES

NOTES

About the author

Patsy Bennett is a rare combination of astrologer and psychic medium. Her horoscopes are published in newspapers and magazines both in Australia and internationally, and she has written freelance for publications including *Nature and Health* and *Practical Parenting*. Patsy has appeared on several live daytime TV and radio shows including *Studio 10* and *The Project*. Her books *Astrology: Secrets of the Moon*, *Your Horoscope for 2020*, the *Astrology Diaries* and the *Zodiac Moon Reading Cards* are published by Rockpool Publishing.

Born in New Zealand, Patsy relocated to the UK where, in the 1980s, she worked as a sub-editor and production editor for women's and fashion magazines including *Woman's Own* and *ELLE* (UK). She studied astrology at the Faculty of Astrological Studies in London in the 1990s and, in 1998, relocated to Australia, where she worked as a reporter for local newspapers in the northern New South Wales area, wrote freelance for magazines and continued her practice as an astrologer.

Patsy has worked as a professional astrologer and medium for over 24 years. She began reading palms and tarot at the age of 14, and experienced mediumistic insights as young as 12. She is a natural medium and has perfected her skill by studying with some of the world's foremost mediums. Patsy provides astrology and psychic intuitive consultations and facilitates astrology and psychic development workshops in northern New South Wales and the Gold Coast.

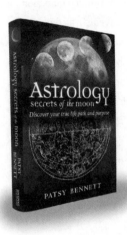

Patsy gained a Master of Arts degree in Romance Languages and Literature at the University of London and taught at the University of California, Berkeley. She is a member of the Queensland Federation of Astrologers and the Spiritualists' National Union.

Patsy runs www.astrocast.com. au, www.patsybennett.com, facebook @patsybennettpsychicastrology and insta@patsybennettastrology.

Further reading of astronomical data

The American Ephemeris for the 21st Century 2000 to 2050, Michelsen, ACS Publications.

Computer programs of astronomical data

Solar Fire, Esoteric Technologies Pty Ltd.

Also by Patsy Bennett

Sun Sign Secrets

Celestial guidance with the sun, moon and stars

ISBN: 9781925946352

This comprehensive, ground-breaking astrology book is for everyone who wants to make the most of their true potential and be in the flow with solar and lunar phases. It includes analyses of each sun sign from Aries to Pisces and pinpoints how you can dynamically make the most of your life in real time alongside celestial events. Work with the gifts and strengths of your sun sign in relation to every lunar phase, zodiacal month, new moon, full moon and eclipse.

Look up your sun sign to read all about your talents and potential pitfalls, and discover how to express your inner star power during the various phases of the sun and moon throughout the days, months and years to come.

Available at all good bookstores.